Danish

Recipes & Reflections

Delectably and *Definitely Danish* Revised

Photo courtesy Museum of Danish America

Museum of Danish America, Elk Horn, Iowa

By Julie Jensen McDonald

Dedications

From *Definitely Danish*

For my granddaughters Erika, Jill, Emily, and Betsy, and for my grandson Eric. There is a quick silver Danishness in them all.

From *Delectably Danish: Recipes and Reflections*

This book is dedicated to my uncle, Marius Jensen, who lights up the lives of everyone at Salem Lutheran Home, Elk Horn, Iowa. He's been enjoying good Danish food for 96 years.

—Julie Jensen McDonald

Front Cover: The Danish open-faced sandwiches were created by the Danish Sisterhood Lodge #3, Davenport, Iowa. Photo by Joan Liffring-Zug Bourret

Back Cover: Photographs by O&H Danish Bakery, Racine, Wisconsin

Acknowledgments:

Beginning in 1993 many people including museum directors add insights to the text in this book. We thank all who contributed to the two titles listed above now merged into *Danish Touches.*

Laura Kath, Media Relations Director,
   Solvang Conference & Visitors Bureau
Staff members of Museum of Danish America
Lisa Riggs, Director Danish Windmill, Elk Horn, Iowa
Gayle Swanson, Concordia Language Villages, Bemidji, Minnesota

Graphic design: M.A. Cook Design

Edited by Whitney Pope, Deb Schense, Jacque Gharib, Melinda Bradnan, and Joan Liffring-Zug Bourret
Line art drawings: Esther Feske (p. 154) only and Diane Heusinkveld
Proverbs: *Danish Proverbs* book available from Penfield Books

Penfield Books, 215 Brown Street, Iowa City, Iowa 52245
www.penfieldbooks.com 1-800-728-9998
© Copyright 2013 Julie Jensen McDonald
Library of Congress Control Number: 2013936223
ISBN-13: 978-1932043389

Contents

About the Author

Julie Jensen McDonald

Amalie's Story is a beautiful novel, the first in a trilogy about Danish Americans, written by Julie Jensen McDonald. This book, originally published by Simon & Schuster in 1970, was followed by *Petra* and finally, *The Sailing Out*, all three based on autobiographical themes in Julie's own Danish-American life. No one else has written a published trilogy based on the large number of Danish-American immigrants and their descendants. Excerpts from these out-of-print titles are in *Forever Danish* published by Penfield Books.

Other Danish titles by Julie include *Danish Proverbs,* still in print, and this book, *Danish Touches* merges two earlier titles, *Delectably Danish: Recipes and Reflections,* and *Definitely Danish* into one book. Her out-of-print book *Scandinavian Proverbs,* a prize-winner, will be released in summer 2013 titled *Scandinavian Wit and Wisdom* with both proverbs and quotations. The proverbs were compiled by Julie; the quotations are compiled by David Wright.

In addition Mrs. McDonald has written a total of sixteen novels. She assisted on Nan Wood Graham's book, *My Brother Grant Wood,* with the late John Zug, and worked with Joan Liffring-Zug Bourret on the book *Grant Wood and Little Sister Nan.* Mrs. McDonald for many years wrote for newspapers in the Quad Cities of Iowa and Illinois. She taught at St. Ambrose University and at the University of Iowa's summer writer's workshop.

Growing Up Danish

When I was a child, I lived in a household where the Danish language was used to thwart "little pitchers with big ears." We understood the tone, if not the words, and we did pick up a few words.

I knew that I was a *lille pige,* I knew that my grandmother was *Bedstemor* and that she was *gammel* (old), and I knew that I couldn't have a bicycle because it was too *dyr.* I also knew a lot of sewing terms that filled the air when my mother, my aunts, and my grandmother were constructing a garment. What I couldn't pick up were the details of the *sladder* (gossip), and this was a great frustration.

As a youngster I assumed that everyone in the world had a life like mine, eating *frikadeller* and *sagosuppe,* celebrating "Little Christmas" before the actual Christmas Day, and knowing for a fact that every baby born for miles around would be white-blond.

Up to a point, the other kids were like me, for this was a town where at least half the phone book was devoted to names ending in "sen."

But there were differences, too. Little by little I noticed that some of the other kids ate meatballs, thought fruit was a weird ingredient for soup—almost as weird as rice in pudding, to say nothing of adding a nut—and welcomed infant siblings who had discernible shocks of dark hair.

The "sen" families were much more American than Danish, but there was still something about them, a sense of deep kinship that we all shared. You simply did not expect rotten behavior from a person named Nielsen, Jensen, or Rasmussen.

Decency was expected of us at home. If we lied, a safety-pin pricked our tongues. We were not permitted to appropriate anything that didn't belong to us—not even a twig from a neighbor's yard. We were not to make others feel "small."

At an early age, I perceived that the Danes possessed a certain sneaky hostility, like tail-wagging dogs that bite. Later I would understand why. They came from a small country, and in the international scheme of things, overt hostility would be suicidal. Their expertise at puncturing the balloons of the powerful reached its zenith during the Nazi occupation.

I quickly devoured the shelf of fairy tales at the public library in Harlan, Iowa, and yearned for more. Any fairy tale was fine, but Hans Christian Andersen's stories seemed best. They had a special pathos that made their magic stronger. I wondered how this man could have come from a nation of butter-and-eggs practicality. How could there be time to spin tales when there was so much work to do? I knew about the work, because my grandmother often told us how she cared for the sheep as a child, knitting constantly as she watched the flock. She never stopped working even when she was old.

That was the thing about being Danish—longevity. Two old men in our town named Chris were prime examples. They were called "Humpy Chris" and "Curly Chris" to keep them straight, but straight was no word for "Humpy Chris." His back curved as if he perpetually carried a sack of potatoes on his shoulders. Both men lived to be nearly a hundred and kept their wits to the end. Women did even better, it seemed. My grandmother said it was because they ate so much barley. To this day, when someone suggests that eighty is a ripe old age, I snort, remembering the *gammel* Danes of my youth.

A Brief History of Denmark

*From an article by Erik Kjersgaard for the Royal Danish
Ministry of Cultural Affairs*

Traces of human habitation from 200,000 years ago have been found, but there is no evidence of any continuity in such settlements. Almost the entire area of what was to become Denmark was covered with ice, exterminating all life until the ice slowly melted around 12,000 B.C.

Agriculture came to Denmark from the south around 4000 B.C. The inhabitants burned off the woods and forests, sowed grain in the ashes, and congregated in villages. By 500 B.C., the country was quite thickly populated, and almost all regions were under cultivation.

Denmark indirectly received powerful impulses from the spread of Roman and Hellenistic culture as well as from the political and military upheavals that led to the decline of the Roman Empire. A wealthy warrior class emerged from a series of battles and skirmishes for control over steadily larger areas of the country. Around A.D. 500 a tribe calling themselves Danes migrated from Sweden with the declared intent of taking possession of what is now Denmark. Their language, passed on to us in a handful of writings, was a northern German dialect, but already easily distinguishable from German itself.

Denmark remained on the outer perimeter of Europe until about A.D. 800, when Charlemagne extended the power of his Franks to what is now northern Germany, where he forcibly converted the population to Christianity. A Danish King, Godfred, took up the challenge and staked out the boundaries of his country, but over the next few decades, the Franks managed to push northward, combining brief military campaigns with Christian missions.

The Viking expeditions in western and central Europe undertaken by the Scandinavians of the period should be seen as counter-offensives to Frankish advances. In only one technical respect did the Vikings have the upper hand: They built and sailed fast, seaworthy warships. This enabled them to rule the North Sea, the Baltic Sea, and adjacent Continental rivers for long periods.

Around A.D. 900, a Norwegian chieftain named Hardegon obtained a firm foothold on the Jutland peninsula, and a couple of generations later his grandson, Harald Bluetooth (950–85) boasted of having "conquered Denmark and made the Danes Christians." Under Harald's son, Sweyn

Forkbeard (985–1014) and grandson, Canute the Great (1019–35), the warrior Viking era culminated in the conquest of England. However, this supremacy was short-lived, and European feudal states soon learned to defend themselves against further attacks.

Canute's nephew, Sweyn Estridsen (1047–74), whose Viking career had been a sad fiasco, began to restructure the Danish monarchy along Continental lines and reorganize the Danish Church, which until then had been a very primitive institution. In 1104, Denmark established a separate national Church, independent of Hamburg. However, imperial influence persisted, fanning internal strife among claimants to the Danish throne until in 1157, Valdemar the Great, assumed absolute and undisputed control of the kingdom.

The Scandinavian Union

Valdemar the Great (1157–82) and his immediate successors consolidated royal power with the help of the clergy and the nobility. Culturally, Denmark became fully integrated with Central Europe and then expanded by making conquests among the Slav and Baltic peoples on the southern and eastern coasts of the Baltic. However, German vassals of Valdemar the Victorious (1202–41) rebelled and seized the initiative from Danish hands, after which the Baltic Sea and neighboring waters remained under domination of the German Hanseatic League for three centuries.

After the frustration of Danish foreign policy aims there followed protracted internal struggles between the crown, the church, and the nobility, and an early fourteenth-century attempt to make new conquests in Northern Germany backfired badly. A shortage of money forced the monarchy to mortgage the nation's castles to German mercenary generals. After Christopher II's reign (1320–26 and 1330–32), he died in 1332. Denmark spent eight years without a king. Christopher's son, Valdemar Atterdag (1340–75) reclaimed the throne, exploited a latent distrust of foreigners among his people, reestablished his kingdom, and secured its gates. Dynastic difficulties caused Valdemar's daughter, Margrethe I, who was queen of Norway, to take over effective control of Denmark as well (from 1375 to 1412), and when the Swedish nobles rebelled against their own German-born king and requested Danish assistance, Denmark, Norway, and Sweden were brought together in 1397 in a union against Germany. The bond between Denmark and Norway was to survive until 1814.

Margrethe's successor, Erik of Pomerania (1412–39) exhausted the resources of the united countries in a desperate attempt to oust the counts of Holstein, who had taken possession of the Danish frontier duchy of Slesvig in the south of Jutland. Sweden withdrew from the union, whereupon the Danish nobility deposed Erik. His successor died without issue in 1448, after which the crowns of both Denmark and Norway passed to Christian I (1448–81). A few years later, Christian was acclaimed as count of Holstein and duke of Slesvig. Frontier disputes over Slesvig were at an end, and Holstein remained united with Denmark for the next 400 years.

The Reformation

Kings Hans (1481–1513) and Christian II (1513–23) both fought on two fronts: They wanted to reestablish the Dano-Swedish union even if it meant going to war, and both tried hard to break the economic stranglehold of the Hanseatic towns. In the former endeavor they were unsuccessful, but discovery of the sea route to India and to the Americas shifted the emphasis in foreign trade from the Baltic to the Atlantic, thereby undermining Hanseatic supremacy. Christian II, a man of vigor and violence, was deposed by a rebellious nobility, and there followed a period during which social and religious tension intensified as the Reformation spread north from Germany. A civil war in 1536 ended with the defeat of both burghers and peasants, and brought about the downfall of the Catholic bishops, whose property was confiscated by the Crown, whereafter the Danish Lutheran Church was placed under the personal control of the king. The temporal nobility was the only group of leaders left to share power with the monarch.

Wars Against Sweden

The dwindling power of the Hanseatic League meant that Denmark and Sweden were free to fight for control of the Baltic Sea. For a generation or two Denmark straddled the Baltic approaches, thereby retaining its economic and military supremacy. Thanks to a gratifying export market for agricultural produce, both landowners and merchants were able to make handsome profits. Many of Denmark's principal Renaissance buildings survive to remind us of the affluence and lavish spending of the nobility of the period. The personal drive of Christian IV (1588–1648) encouraged the flowering of architecture, painting, music, and the national economy.

Sweden, however, having long exerted control over Finland, managed to gain supremacy in the inner Baltic from the Gulf of Finland in the north to Gdansk in the south. In 1625, Christian IV, in the hope of neutralizing Swedish expansion, entered the Thirty Years' War against the Catholic League. His defeat was complete, and in addition he had to suffer the ignominy of seeing his Swedish rival, Gustavus Adolphus, triumph as the great Protestant general in Germany, a role he himself had coveted. A head-on collision with Sweden in the king's later years resulted in the loss of certain positions in the Baltic.

In 1657, Frederik III felt it was time to take some measure of revenge on the Swedes, but the Danish army was routed by the enemy. Only grim defense of the capital, Copenhagen, prevented the entire country from falling into the hands of the Swedish king. The territorial losses, however, were bitter enough, consisting as they did of all the old Danish provinces in southern Sweden and the island of Bornholm.

The conclusion of hostilities found Denmark in a state of grave economic and national crisis. Bold measures were necessary. In 1660, with the support of the army and citizens of Copenhagen, Frederik III brought off a coup d'etat through which he virtually deprived the nobility of their privileges, including their right to govern. In a difficult situation, the new absolutist government implemented a series of administrative reforms and took steps to reorganize the country's defenses. The result was sufficiently successful to permit Denmark to put up a reasonable fight in subsequent wars with Sweden (1675–79, 1699–1700, and 1709–20), although the former Danish territories in southern Sweden (with the exception of Bornholm) were never regained.

Reforms

Over the next eighty years, Denmark and Norway remained neutral in all international conflicts, which helped to consolidate foreign trade and gave the two countries an economic boost. In 1784, the future Frederick VI, as a sixteen-year-old crown prince, assumed control, and general affluence provided a basis for both technical and social reforms. The long-suffering peasant class was granted civil rights, and the rigid social pattern based on the village was dissolved. Peasants were no longer obliged to remain in prescribed geographical areas, and were free to buy or rent land and farm it for themselves. Education was made compulsory for all children, and illiteracy was eradicated.

British Attacks

The French Revolution in 1789 produced little more than a ripple in Denmark, but Napoleon's increasing power on the Continent and Britain's quite unfounded fear that the Danish government might be induced to place its fleet at the disposal of the French unleashed British attacks in 1801 and 1807. Copenhagen was bombarded and the Danish fleet was seized as British spoil. The attack on Copenhagen forced the Danish government into an alliance with France, which continued until Napoleon's fall in 1814. When Sweden joined the allied powers and demanded that Denmark cede Norway to the Swedes, the Danish government was powerless to protest. Only the ancient Norse possessions in the Atlantic, namely the Faeroe Islands, Iceland, and Greenland, remained united with Denmark.

The years following 1814 were dark, dismal, and lean, but cultural life flourished with writers like Adam Oehlenschläger and Hans Christian Andersen, the painter C.W. Eckersberg, the sculptor Bertel Thorvaldsen, the architect C.F. Hansen, the composer C.E.F. Weyse, the physicist H.C. Ørsted, the philologist Rasmus Rask, the philosopher Søren Kierkegaard, the archaeologist C.D. Thomsen, and the versatile ballet master August Bournonville. At the same time, theologian N.F.S. Grundtvig was demonstrating the power of his writing by inspiring a popular religious and national revival.

A libertarian constitution drawn up for Denmark in 1849 extended such a broad franchise that overnight Denmark became far and away the most democratic country in Europe. However, a constitution including Denmark and Slesvig, but excluding Holstein, prompted Germany to place Holstein under military occupation. The Prussian Prime Minister, Otto van Bismarck, declared war in 1864. Slesvig was lost, and for more than fifty years the area remained a German possession.

The loss of Holstein, the most industrialized region in the realm, obliged the remainder of the country to increase industrial production. Many light industries and a handful of heavier ones were established, including breweries, sugar refineries, shipyards, and cement manufacturing plants, the latter being one of the very few industries for which raw materials could be obtained from the Danish subsoil. Eventually, however, farmers got together to form cooperatives, regional dairies, and bacon factories, and agriculture became Denmark's largest industry.

After World War I, the northern part of Slesvig, following a plebiscite in accordance with the Treaty of Versailles, was reunited with Denmark, while Iceland was recognized as an independent, sovereign state and in personal union with Denmark, with a common head of state and foreign policy.

World War II brought another declaration of neutrality from Denmark, but the country was occupied in connection with Nazi Germany's campaign to take Norway. Denmark joined NATO in 1949. In 1952, Denmark, Finland, Iceland, Norway, and Sweden formed the Nordic Council, an assembly of parliamentarians which works on various fronts to promote relations between the Nordic countries. By the mid-1960s the value of industrial exports exceeded that of agricultural exports.

Individual material affluence became greater than ever before, and as a result of the liberation of women during the 1970s, women swarmed onto the labor market, so that during the 1980s, the woman without a job away from home was a rarity in Denmark.

A major question posed by the free internal market of the European Economic Community is how the many relatively small Danish businesses, which admittedly excel in fields such as design, research, and inventiveness, will manage to survive when capital is allowed to flow freely and conditions for competition will be the same from Scotland to Gibraltar.

Storks build nests on rooftops in Northern Europe.

Danish Royalty

The history of the royal family of Denmark, Europe's oldest, began with King Gorm the Old, who left his mark on the famous Jelling Stone in Jutland. The inscription reads, "King Gorm erected this memorial to Tyra, his wife, glory of Denmark." Gorm died before 950, and his son, Harald Bluetooth, succeeded him. King Harald's most momentous act was allowing himself to be baptized into the Christian faith. Harald's son, Svend Forkbeard, followed him on the throne, but did not become a Christian.

More than a thousand years stretched between the reign of King Gorm and that of Queen Margrethe II, and fifty-three monarchs have occupied the Danish throne. The kings have included three Haralds, two Svends, six Knuds, two Olufs, seven Eriks, four Valdemars, three Christophers, ten Christians, nine Fredericks, one Abel, one Magnus, one Gorm, and one John. Unannounced in advance, King Frederik IX, a six-foot-six-inch pianist, often wielded the baton as an orchestra conductor in Copenhagen. Caring little for the trappings of royalty, he liked to ride his bicycle around the city.

His daughter, Queen Margrethe, is the second of that name and also the second woman to rule Denmark. In 1953, the Danes voted to eliminate their constitution's provision for male-only succession, and Queen Margrethe recalls her relief. She says she thought, "Oh, I can stay all my life in Denmark." Many princesses marry royalty and go elsewhere, as did the queen's younger sisters, Benedikte, who married a German prince, and Anne-Marie, who lives in England as the exiled Queen of Greece.

Queen Margrethe was born April 16, 1940, a week after the Nazi invasion of Denmark. Although she lived in Amalienborg Palace, Margrethe's childhood was not too different from that of other Danish children. As a teenager, she answered to the nickname "Daisy," and she became known for her sly, self-deprecating wit. Incidentally, no one even blinked an eye at a future queen acquiring a nickname that is in the English language. Nearly all Danes speak both Danish and English, and many know other languages as well.

According to a widely repeated story, a public school classmate said to her, "My name's Bente. What's yours?"

"Margrethe."

"What does your father do?" Bente asked.

"He's a king. What's yours?"

Margrethe grew tall, like her father, but she stopped at six feet. She may be the world's best educated monarch, having studied at the University of Copenhagen, the University of Aarhus, London School of Economics, Cambridge, and the Sorbonne. Her studies were in politics, economics, and archeology. She speaks five languages.

A Danish diplomat echoed the pride of the Danes when he said, "Our queen has a brain." Among her accomplishments are painting, embroidery, and working in porcelain. She designed the scenery and costumes for a television production of H.C. Andersen's *The Shepherdess and the Chimney Sweep* and for the Royal Danish Ballet. She illustrated the Danish edition of Tolkien's *The Lord of the Rings,* and she and her husband translated Simone de Beauvoir into Danish.

The queen's husband, Henri de Laborde de Monpezat, is a former French diplomat who for her sake changed his name to Henrik, renounced his Catholicism, and became a Lutheran. They have two sons, Prince Frederik, born May 26, 1968, and Prince Joachim, born June 7, 1969.

A Copenhagen publisher once said, "Having a monarch spares us the need of having a president." In the past, other Danes have said, "We give our king unlimited power, provided he doesn't use any of it." Queen Margrethe's power is limited to signing laws passed by the parliament, but her lifestyle has a powerful effect on her fellow citizens.

Margrethe took the throne January 12, 1972, upon the death of her father. She declined many titles claimed by her predecessors, asking to be known simply as the Queen of Denmark.

The queen made her first state visit to the United States in February 1991 with Prince Henrik. At the National Museum of Women in Arts in Washington, D.C., she unveiled a Danish exhibit in which her own work was represented.

The royal couple attended a Bournonville Ballet performed by dancers with Danish connections, and the premiere of a play based on Isak Dinesen's story, *Lucifer's Child,* starring Julie Harris.

When Margrethe II became Queen of Denmark, she said, "I hope people will remember me as the one who did her best, and who wasn't an anachronism."

The Lure of the North

Danes seem particularly susceptible to the siren story of the North, and several of them have earned fame for their Arctic explorations. Christian IV, the sailor king of Denmark, dispatched four expeditions to Greenland and in 1619, he commissioned Jens Munk to search for the Northwest Passage from Hudson Bay into the western seas.

When Munk was a small child, his father was jailed for misusing public funds, and the boy was forced to grow up in a hurry. At the age of eleven, he went to Portugal for a year to learn the language, and met some of the richest merchants in the world. At thirteen, he slipped aboard a Dutch vessel for Brazil, and on the return voyage, a French squadron sank his ship. He made his way back to Bahia, Brazil, and worked as a shoemaker's apprentice.

When Munk was eighteen, two Dutch vessels entered the Bahia harbor, and Portuguese authorities planned to seize them. Munk's employer sent him to warn the Dutch, and he went home with them. He returned to Copenhagen, where he became a merchant captain and owned his own vessel at the age of twenty-five. The North beckoned, and he sailed to Iceland, the Barents Sea, and an island north of Russia. In 1617, Munk established the first Danish whaling enterprise in Spitsbergen waters.

Munk's 1619 expedition to Hudson Bay sailed on two ships, the Unicorn and the Lamprey. By mid-July, they were being buffeted by ice in the Strait of Hudson. Finally, the ice immobilized them.

The first seaman died August 8, and sickness spread by early September. They shot a polar bear for food, and they also shot ptarmigan and hares as long as the snow was not too deep. On November 27, a sharp freeze shattered all glass bottles on the ships. One of the two surgeons on the exhibition died December 12, and it was too cold to go ashore to bury him.

More deaths were imminent: Rasmus Jensen, the minister, and the second surgeon took to their beds January 10. The head cook died that day. By January 21, thirteen were sick. The surgeon was still alive but unable to tell Munk what the medicines were. The labels were all in Latin, and the dead minister had always read them for him.

By late January, even tin pots were bursting in the cold, and the deaths continued. Munk's March 30 journal entry reads, "At this time commenced my greatest sorrow and misery, and I was then like a wild and lonely bird. I was now obliged myself to run about in the ship, to give drink to the sick, to boil drink for them, and get for them what I thought might be good for them, to which I was not accustomed, of which I had but little knowledge."

The description of the fatal ailment would indicate that it was scurvy, and by June 4, only three men and Munk remained alive. Their teeth were too loose to chew any food they might come by. Sixty-one had died, but the few men that remained got the ships free of the ice and set sail for home on July 16. They sighted the coast of Norway on September 20. Having endured such hardships, wouldn't a prudent man keep to more southerly latitudes? Jens Munk wanted to return to the Northwest and carry out his mission. However, the Thirty Years' War was now under way, and King Christian needed him for something else. He became an Admiral of the Danish Fleet in 1628, but he never forgot the unconquerable North.

Vitus Bering served another monarch, Peter the Great of Russia, who sought to determine where the Czar's lands joined America and to determine what could be made of that unexplored territory.

Bering was born in Horsens, Jutland, in 1681. His father was not well-off and had many children, so Vitus Bering was on his own at an early age. He joined the Russian fleet when he was twenty-two.

For the 1724 expedition, Bering's lieutenants included Martin Spanberg, another Dane. They began their journey by crossing Russia and Siberia to Kamchatka, where they built their ship, the Fortune. It was christened in June 1725.

What Peter really had in mind was dominion over North America, but he didn't tell this to Bering. When Bering reached a point off the coast of Chukotsk Peninsula where it turns west, he concluded that he had proved the separation of Asia and America. Bering Strait was discovered August 11, 1728.

Russian authors have compared Bering to Columbus. Through his efforts, a great continent was scientifically explored, and the Arctic coast, the longest in the world, was charted. A new route to the western world was found.

Peter Freuchen, born in Denmark in 1886, studied to be a doctor, but the genes of a seafaring grandfather were too strong to resist. He went to Greenland for the first time as a ship's stoker, and he had a way of ingratiating himself with the Innuits (Eskimos) that led to his eventual marriage to one.

His detailed description of their ways included the information that an Innuit beauty washed her hair in urine before a big dance. The liquid was often used for tanning hides and for cleansing purposes. Freuchen's bride learned to appreciate bathing. She became a famous hostess in their Greenland settlement.

Freuchen wrote the story of a man whose companion died of natural causes, but the stark loneliness of the North compelled him to pretend his friend was alive. The ground was frozen too hard to bury him, so the corpse was carried in and out. When thawing caused an arm to move, he seemed to be alive, and his friend finished him with a shotgun, only to be charged with murder. That charge was dismissed, but it didn't matter. The "murderer" was hopelessly insane.

Freuchen walked barefoot on the ice and was forever stepping into the frigid waters. He said he didn't feel it, but eventually he lost a leg to the frozen North.

He admired Knud Rasmussen (1879–1933), another Arctic explorer, and told how Rasmussen capsized his kayak harpooning a narwhal whale. Freuchen told him he'd better go home for a change of clothes, and he said, "Don't you see this is our chance for a big killing?" Then Freuchen suggested that he wring his clothes out, at least. Rasmussen asked, "Why?"

The answer was, "Because you're wet as hell!"

Rasmussen responded, "By God, I forgot about that!"

"That's the kind of man who makes a real explorer," Freuchen wrote.

When his own exploring days were done, Freuchen lived in New York City with his third wife, a Danish artist, and wrote books about his adventurous past. He also appeared on a television quiz show. Pipaluk Freuchen, the daughter of Freuchen and his Innuit wife, inherited his literary talent, becoming an author of Danish children's books.

Knud Johan Victor Rasmussen, of whom Freuchen wrote, also wrote of his own expeditions, including *Myths and Legends from Greenland* (1921–25) and *Across Arctic America* (1927). Born in 1879 at Jakobshavn, Greenland, he was part Innuit and spent much of his life with the Innuits, including the world's most northerly tribe, which is in northwest Greenland. In 1910, he established a base and trading post at Thule. In 1912, with three helpers, Rasmussen crossed the Greenland ice sheet to the Northeast coast. He collected the folk stories, songs, and legends of Greenland's Innuits. In 1923–24 he crossed the American Arctic studying the Innuit people throughout northern Canada and Alaska to Point Barrow, Alaska.

Immigration to America

The big push of immigration (nearly 250,000 persons) came between 1850 and 1930. The peak year was 1882 when nearly 12,000 Danes arrived. In times when jobs, land, and opportunities were scarce in Denmark, the New World beckoned in song, story, and poem, to say nothing of the letters written by Danes who had taken the plunge and found prosperity.

In the 1840s and 1850s, there were Danish immigrant groups in cities— New York, Perth Amboy, Hartford, Boston, and Portland. Many moved west into Pennsylvania, Ohio, and Indiana.

Chicago was a major landing point on the Great Lakes. The first Dane came to Racine, Wisconsin, in 1839, and thousands followed. They first made wagons that were driven westward by pioneers. Later, they made auto parts and lawn mowers. The first rural settlement was in 1846 on land near the present town of Hartland, just west of Milwaukee. Immigrants arriving during the next two decades included some Icelanders who were Danish citizens and who settled in Door County.

Of course, a few Danes arrived much earlier. Hans Christian Febiger, who was known as "Old Denmark," came to America via the Virgin Islands, served under George Washington during the American Revolution, and retired as a brigadier general. Christian Guldager, who had won a gold medal at Copenhagen's Academy of Fine Arts, is remembered for his portrait of George Washington and its distinctly Danish nose with a slope and a tilt. Charles Zanco, who fought for Texas freedom, painted the first flag with a five-pointed star in the center. Under the star, Zanco printed the word "Independence." Texas has been the Lone Star State ever since. Zanco died in the battle of the Alamo.

Demark's new constitution of 1849 allowed non-Lutheran worship, but many Baptists and Mormons wanted America's even greater freedom. Mormon missionaries were more successful in Denmark than in any other European country except England. By 1870, more than 20,000 Danish Mormons had emigrated, mostly from northern Jutland, the poorest part of Denmark.

During the Civil War, a small group of Danish Baptists in Wisconsin headed for south-central Minnesota in a covered wagon. Rather than risk the perils of Sioux country further on, they bought land in the Lake Geneva area, which became the home of some of the early cooperative creameries.

In 1866, more Danes left Racine for the prairie near Sleepy Eye, Minnesota.

The restless Danes of Wisconsin pushed on to Minnesota, Dakota Territory, Illinois, Iowa, Nebraska, and Kansas. Some were attracted to Michigan by good wages in the lumber camps, locating in Manistee, Ludington, and Muskegon on Lake Michigan.

In 1885, about seventy members of the Danish Evangelical Lutheran Church founded Tyler in southwestern Minnesota. Later in 1906, Tyler residents and others settled 20,000 acres of burned-over land in northeastern Minnesota, including the present town of Askov. Blasting tree stumps, they planted potatoes. One settler received rutabaga seeds from a friend in Denmark. They thrived, and in the 1950s, farmers around Askov were growing one-fourth of the nation's rutabagas—the "Rutabaga Capital of America."

Between 1880 and 1890, the Danish population of Minneapolis and St. Paul grew more than 700 percent. The new residents found work as laborers and artisans. Their first settlement was along the Mississippi River in South Minneapolis, an area known as the Danish Flats. Later, the concentration was in the west river area as far south as Minnehaha Park.

Danes moved into Dakota Territory in the late 1860s and early 1870s. Northeast of Yankton, they created Viborg, which became the largest Danish colony in the United States in this early period. Among the first citizens were young and middle-aged couples, but many immigrants were unmarried men. Mary Larsen was the first female and the only woman resident of Viborg for several months. In 1893, her brother, W.C. Larsen, built a general store and post office that was promptly flattened by a windstorm. He rebuilt it in a month. A hardware store, a lumber company, a blacksmith shop, a drugstore, a hotel, and a livery stable also came into being in 1893. Soon to follow were a newspaper, the *Viborg Enterprise,* a telephone company, and an electric lighting system. Ole Sorensen, who suggested that the town be named Viborg, promoted a railroad from Sioux Falls to Yankton. Unfortunately, he was buried on the day the first passenger train came to Viborg.

North Dakota's largest settlement is in the northwestern counties of Ward, Renville, and Burke. A landmark in Kenmare is the Danish windmill that ground grain until it was moved into town.

Settlers in Illinois came from the island of Lolland and northern Slesvig. They started farming as renters and soon became landowners. The Danish population always kept to the northern portion of the state, with the heaviest concentration in Chicago.

Once the Danes learned about the rich land in Iowa, they came in great numbers. Holsteiners and German Slesvigers arrived in 1838, settling in the Mississippi River areas of Davenport and Clinton. After 1864, more came because they wanted to escape German rule of their home provinces. The map of Iowa is dotted with Danish settlements.

The largest group of Danes in Nebraska was in Omaha, and in the 1870s and 1880s, eastern and central Nebraska had numerous settlements. The town of Dannebrog, north of Intestate 80 and Grand Island, was named for the Danish flag, and settlers established a Danish newspaper, *Stjernen* "Star." Danish and American flags fly daily on Main Street, and the Nebraska State Legislature proclaimed Dannebrog the "Danish Capital of Nebraska."

Some settlers chose Mirage Flats, rich land bordering the Niobrara River in northwest Nebraska, where they lived in soddies or dugouts while they built houses. It was as if they could foresee the irrigation of the future that would make this land bloom.

Danes settled in Missouri, but they were not numerous. The Kansas settlements were more prosperous, but on May 30, 1869, sixty Native Americans swooped down, killing five people at one settlement. Danish Socialists started a Utopian colony near Hays City, Kansas, but after six weeks of hard work and quarreling, they sold the property and divided the assets.

Utah had seen an influx in Mormon Danes, and in northeast Montana, Emil Ferdinand Madsen founded the Dagmar Colony and built himself a castle-like home.

About 1830, Christian Hillebrandt, a native of Sleswig-Holstein, after nearly ten years of raising cattle in Louisiana, moved west and raised cattle on more than 20,000 acres of land in southeast Texas. By the time of the Civil War, a Texas area northeast of Austin was being settled by Danish farm families and became a part of Lee County known as "Little Denmark."

In 1895, the first of more than seventy families arrived to found a Danish colony in Texas near the Gulf coast southwest of Houston. Many of them came from the Kimballton, Iowa, area. They raised cotton and longhorn cattle. Almost overwhelmed when the land flooded, they stuck it out, building levees to keep their fields from turning to mud during the heavy rains. These families were members of the Danish Evangelical Lutheran Church, the "Happy Danes" of N.F.S. Grundtvig, whose son, F.L. Grundtvig, visited the community in its early years. It became Danevang, south of El Campo. A display at the famed Institute of Texan Cultures in San Antonio honors the Texas Danes.

The lure of the Pacific Northwest drew many Danes, a number of whom had first settled in the Midwest. The first European to settle in Washington state was Matts Petersen, who staked his 160 acres in 1865. Danish immigrants established many dairy farms. Some individual farmers delivered milk house-to-house in Seattle and other cities. Other Danes were in logging. Peter Larsen constructed major portions of the Northern Pacific and other railroads. Hans Pedersen, born in Denmark, built Seattle hotels, streets, the King County Courthouse, the Seattle Ford Motor plant, and handled many other construction projects.

The Nordic Heritage Museum in Seattle has five 1,000-square-foot galleries, one each for Denmark, Finland, Sweden, Norway, and Iceland. Another gallery focuses on the fishing and logging industries of the Northwest, and two rooms display costumes, textiles, tools, and other belongings of the settlers.

Wherever they settled, the Danes enthusiastically appropriated the American Dream, and "there were very few rogues among them." A leavening of Danes was an excellent thing for a new country.

Fulfilling Expectations in America

One of the best known Danes in America is Victor Borge. Interrupting his piano concerts with his comedy routine, Borge deliberately frustrates listeners who want to hear more of his music, but he delights those who enjoy his clever plays on words. A star in Denmark and other European countries, Borge targeted Hitler and other Nazi leaders with his jokes. On the day that the Nazis invaded Denmark, April 9, 1940, Borge was performing in Sweden. Marked for death for his anti-Hitler wisecracks and because he is a Jew (Borge Rosenbaum), Borge could not go back to Denmark. He came to America, where his appearance on Bing Crosby's weekly Kraft Music Hall radio show was so well received that he appeared on the show once a week for more than a year. He joked about the English language as he improved his English. Thus if he didn't like today's forecast, he might "check the five-cast" and see if it was better. Audiences were pleased by his fresh outlook. Borge founded "Thanks to Scandinavia," an organization that helps young Scandinavians come to study in America.

Lauritz Melchior, born in Copenhagen in 1890, first sang as a boy soprano. He studied at the Royal Opera School. Combined study and performances at the Bayreuth Festivals established him as a leading Wagnerian tenor. From 1926 to 1950, he sang Wagnerian roles at the Metropolitan Opera in New York.

Jean Hersholt, best known for his "Dr. Christian" radio character, appeared in more than 200 films including "Greed," "Stella Dallas," and "The Mask of Fu Manchu." He received special Academy Awards for philanthropic efforts for actors. Hersholt became an American citizen in 1918, but he maintained close ties with the homeland. He was active in the Danish war relief after World War II. His extensive collection of Hans Christian Andersen material was given to the Library of Congress "in gratitude for what this country has meant for me and my family."

Buddy Ebsen, another entertainer with that special Danish twinkle, starred in television shows including "Davy Crockett," "The Beverly Hillbillies," and "Barnaby Jones." Ebsen started as a dancer in Broadway shows and Hollywood musicals. His younger sister Vilma often performed with him in the 1930s.

Libby Larsen, granddaughter of a Danish immigrant, has been a composer-in-residence with the Minnesota Orchestra, which premiered her symphony, "Water Music," in 1985. She has written a two-act romantic opera and a choral symphony, "Coming Forth Into Day," with a text created in collaboration with Jehan el-Sadat, the widow of Anwar Sadat, Egypt's assassinated president.

Danish-American artists include Carl Christian Anton Christensen, a Mormon who painted scenes of Mormon history, and Peter Gui Clausen, who is known for Minnesota frontier scenes. Ferdinand Reichardt of Minnesota has two paintings in the White House—one an upper Mississippi River landscape. Olaf Wieghorst, who painted Western scenes, has four paintings in the collection of former President and Mrs. Ronald Reagan. Wieghorst acted in two John Wayne films.

Carl Rohl-Smith and Johanes Gelert, Danish-born sculptors, gained fame in this country. Rohl-Smith's best-known works are two pieces commemorating General William Tecumseh Sherman and Iowa veterans of the Civil War. Gelert is remembered for his statue of Hans Christian Andersen in Chicago's Lincoln Park, and for his statue, which is in the Police Academy, of a Chicago policeman, memorializing police killed in the 1886 Haymarket riot.

Sculptor Christian Petersen, who arrived in America at the age of nine, came to what is now Iowa State University in 1934 to create sculptures for the Dairy Industry building and remained to become the first artist-in-residence at Iowa State. His last work—created before his death in 1960—is an eight-foot sculpture in the reflecting lake at the Fisher Community Center, Marshalltown, Iowa, of a father holding his small son high "to symbolize this generation helping the next generation to see beyond what has been able to see...so the child is looking into the future, having a little more light."

Writers with a Danish sensibility include Enok Mortensen, who wrote novels, short stories, and history in both Danish and English. Mortensen was a mainstay at Danebrod Camps in Tyler, Minnesota, and was active in organizing the Danish Immigrant Archives at Grand View University in Des Moines, Iowa.

One of the first to write in English was Sophus Keith in Winther, who was born in Denmark and came with his parents to Weeping Water, Nebraska, at the age of two. Educated at the University of Washington, he was a member of the English faculty there until 1963. His works include a critical study of Eugene O'Neill and a trilogy about immigrant farmers in Nebraska, *Take All To Nebraska, Mortgage Your Heart,* and *This Passion Never Dies.* Perhaps the trilogy form is necessary to trace the Danish presence in America. I used the trilogy form to tell the story of the Jorgen family, Danish immigrants in Iowa: *Amalie's Story, Petra,* and *The Sailing Out.* (A fourth novel is titled *Reaching*). Dr. Peter L. Petersen of the West Texas State University history faculty offers a clear and concise overview in his book, *The Danes in America.*

Danes have been active in public life. Frederick Valdemar Peterson was governor of Nebraska from 1947 to 1953 and later was U.S. Ambassador to Denmark and Finland. Ben Jensen was an Iowa congressman for thirteen terms. During World War II, he helped the Office of War Information to prepare Danish-language shortwave broadcasts to occupied Denmark. In 1954, when Puerto Rican extremists opened fire on the House of Representatives, Jensen was one of five congressmen wounded.

The grandparents of Lloyd Bentsen, the U.S. senator from Texas who became President Clinton's Secretary of the Treasury, lived in South Dakota. The family moved to the Rio Grande Valley in 1918 and bought the low-priced land that built their fortune in citrus and other crops. President Clinton's Attorney General, Janet Reno, is of Danish descent.

Ancher Nelsen of Minnesota administered the U.S. Rural Electrification Program, served in Congress, and represented the United States at the funeral of King Frederik IX of Denmark in 1972.

A former member of the U. S. House of Representatives, Jim Nussle of

Iowa, whose grandfather came from Denmark, opposed excessive spending and once covered his head with a paper bag with eye holes to protest a congressional check-bouncing scandal.

Because his true love's family would not permit their marriage, Jacob Riis, born in Ribe in 1849, and his sweetheart had their happy ending in America, where Riis became a reporter for the *New York Tribune* and the *Evening Sun,* writing about the plight of the poor in New York tenements. His photographs were even more powerful than his words. He was one of the first to use flash, capturing the interiors of the dismal dwellings. His book, *How the Other Half Lives,* created a sensation in 1890.

John Hansen came to America early in the century with little more than the clothes on his back and founded the Hansaloy Company of Davenport, Iowa, which produced some of the first blades for slicing bread.

Niels Poulson came to America at age 21 to work as a bricklayer. He became an architectural draftsman and created what became the Hecla Architectural Iron Works. Its products were used in constructing New York's Grand Central and Pennsylvania stations. In 1910 to 1911, Poulson gave $600,000 to the American Scandinavian Foundation.

In 1901, William Petersen came to the United States at the age of 21 and worked as a blacksmith. As the need for horseshoeing declined, he invented what he named a "Vise-Grip," with a locking lever, producing thousands of them a day in De Witt, Nebraska.

"Big Bill" Knudsen, born in Copenhagen in 1879 as Signius Wilhelm Poul, arrived in New York in 1900 with $30 and climbed the auto industry ladder to become a famed president of General Motors Corporation. In World War II, he was one of the dollar-a-year men helping the government. His assignment was to develop defense production programs. Knudsen became a lieutenant general in 1942, the only civilian in American history appointed to that high a rank. Big Bill's son, Sermon Emil or "Bunkie," followed his father's auto career, becoming president of Chevrolet and of Ford Motor Company.

Max Henius, born in Aalborg, emigrated in 1886 and eventually formed Wahl & Henius, chemists who served brewers all over the world. Henius identified the source of a typhoid epidemic that threatened Chicago in 1892 as milk diluted with polluted water from Lake Michigan. He was one of the founders of Rebild National Park in Denmark.

Peter Jensen, born in Denmark, teamed up with Edwin S. Pridham to develop a high fidelity horn loudspeaker, testing their "Magnavox" (great voice) at a San Francisco football game in 1915. He also founded Jensen Radio Manufacturing Company. His enterprises were the foundations of the high fidelity industry.

Niels Hansen, whose family came to America in 1873 when he was seven, became a horticulturist at South Dakota State College and the Agricultural Experiment Station in Brookings, South Dakota, developing new varieties of crops to withstand the climate of the Northern Plains. His creations included hybrid varieties of apples, apricots, pears, and plums.

Jens Jensen, who became a famous landscape artist, ran away to America with his sweetheart in 1884. Jensen became superintendent and landscape architect of the entire West Chicago Park system. He developed the first neighborhood park, landscaped Luther College at Decorah, Iowa, and Henry Ford's Dearborn estate, and opened a school for landscape architects in Door County, Wisconsin, teaching there until his death in 1951 at age ninety-one.

When it comes to "big" achievements, no one outranks "Dinosaur Jim" Jensen. In 1972, Jensen discovered the largest known dinosaur (two shoulder blades each eight feet long) only to find, seven years later, a nine-foot-long shoulder blade, or scapula, just thirty feet from the original site, the Dry Mesa Quarry in southwestern Colorado. These were the bones of giant creatures—perhaps fifty feet in height and 100 feet long—that roamed the earth 150 million years ago. When Jensen retired as director of the Earth Science Museum of Brigham Young University in Provo, Utah, he left uncounted tons of dinosaur bones stored beneath the stands of the University's football stadium to await study. Jensen was born August 2, 1918 in Leamington in central Utah.

His father, a naturalist, introduced him to fossils and gave him a college text when Jim was twelve years old. Jim Jensen first dug for fossils near the family farm. After high school, he made his first trip to Alaska, where he found Ice Age horse bones. He later looked for ancient bones throughout the world. In Antarctica he discovered bones of a mammal-like reptile identical to others located in Africa and Asia—important to the proof of Continental Drift. Jensen taught ceramics and pottery, painted the portraits of more than 1,000 Native Americans, and served on the staff of the Museum of Comparative Zoology at Harvard University.

There are many memorable Danish Americans, particularly in Hollywood. Actresses Jessica Alba, Jamie Lee Curtis, Eliza Dushku, Scarlett Johanson, and Mary-Kate and Ashley Olsen are of Danish descent. Actors

Hayden Christiansen, Buddy Ebsen, Jean Hersholt, Viggo Mortensen, Leslie Nielsen, and Elijah Wood also come from Danish ancestry.

The drummer for the band Metallica, Lars Ulrich, was born in Gentofte, Denmark, and immigrated to America in 1980.

The all-time leading scorer in NFL history, Morten Andersen, was born in Copenhagen and is nicknamed "The Great Dane." Oscar Mathæus Nielsen, also known as Battling Nelson or "the Durable Dane," was a Danish-American boxer who held the world lightweight championship twice. One of the NBA's first power forwards in the 1950s, Vern Mikkelsen, grew up in Askov, Minnesota, a town of primarily Danish Americans.

Steny Hoyer, House Majority Leader from 2007 to 2011, has Danish heritage on his father's side.

William Webster Hansen, born to a Danish immigrant, was one of the founders of the technology of microwave electronics. Danish-American biochemist, Max Henius, specialized in the fermentation process and cofounded the American Academy of Brewing in Chicago. Holger Thiele, son of noted Danish astronomer, Thorvald Nicolai Thiele, discovered several asteroids and comets. Jens Christen Clausen, a pioneer in the field of ecological and evolutionary genetics of plants, was born in Eskilstrup, Denmark.

Additionally, the only male on the list of the top ten oldest verified persons in history, Christian Mortensen, was born to the son of a tailor in the village of Skårup, Denmark. He was born August 16, 1882, and died April 25, 1998; he was 115 years and 252 days old. Mortensen is the oldest immigrant on record, immigrating to the United States in 1903.

All of these Danish Americans attest to the influence of strong individuals from a small country on the vast nation that is America.

SHARED
SORROW
IS HALF
SORROW.

Danish Proverb
H.C. Anderson Paper Cut

Hans Christian Andersen paper cut from
Penfield Books in postcard or magnet.

Names for Babies

Americans of Danish descent looking for names for their children may be discouraged by the way they sound. In English, for example, "Dagmar" sounds like "drag far," but in Danish it is a soft "Dow-mer" with the accent on the first syllable. In Danish, Rigmor has the pleasant sound of "Ree-mor." Here are some names:

Names for Girls

Abelone	Elisabeth	Johanne	Marie
Agnes	Ellen	Juliane	Marna
Andrea	Else	Julie	Mette
Anna	Emma	Katrine	Petra
Anne	Gerda	Kirstine	Rigmor
Camilla	Gunhild	Lene	Sara
Cecillia	Helga	Laura	Signe
Christina	Hilda	Louise	Sigrid
Christine	Ingrid	Maren	Sine
Dagmar	Ingeborg	Margrethe	Sofie
Edith	Jensine	Maria	

Names for Boys

Aage	Erik	Karl	Nicolaj
Anders	Eskild	Kasper	Niels
Andreas	Espen	Knud	Ole
Anton	Frederik	Lars	Peder
Axel	Henrik	Laurs	Peter
Bertel	Jans	Laurits	Poul
Carl	Iver	Mads	Rasmus
Chresten	Jakob	Martin	Sofus
Christen	Jens	Mathies	Søren
Christian	Johan	Mikkel	Svend
Ejner	Jonas	Morten	Valdemar
Emil	Jørgen	Nils	Viktor

And many others. It's unlikely that you'd choose the first name of Gutzon Borglum, the sculptor of Mount Rushmore, but that one sounds better in Danish, too—"Goot-sun."

Incidentally, some Danes today use hyphenated surnames, such as Erik Bohé-Jørgensen and Jens Glysing-Jensen.

The Museum of Danish America

Previously known as The Danish Immigrant Museum
Elk Horn, Iowa
Celebrating Danish Roots and American Dreams!
Mission Statement, adopted June 2011

The Museum of Danish America was founded in 1983 and opened a 16,000 square foot building to the public in 1994. Several thousand visitors come to the museum in person every year; through traveling exhibitions, outreach programs, events, and online resources the museum reaches an additional 100,000 people annually. Core exhibitions tell the story of immigrants from Denmark and ongoing relations between Denmark and the United States. Several changing exhibitions every year highlight artists, historical events, and many different aspects of Danish and Danish-American culture. As the only museum dedicated to the national story of Danish Americans, the museum has collected a diversity of artifacts from across the country and spanning several centuries. For most of the museum's 40,000 pieces in the artifact, archival, and photograph collections, the individual items preserve a story of people or families that are part of a mosaic of Danish-American experiences. Many of those artifacts are stored behind glass walls to allow visitors to see them in Visible Storage. By celebrating the specific culture and history of Danish immigrants and their descendants, the museum contributes to a broader celebration of ethnic diversity in the United States. The museum is located in Elk Horn, Iowa, which lies in the center of the largest concentration of individuals claiming Danish ancestry. The community was the site of the first Danish American Folk High School, founded in 1878, and it reaffirmed its Danish roots in 1976 by purchasing a windmill in Denmark and re-erecting it in Elk Horn as a bicentennial project. Moreover the community lies midway between Des Moines and Omaha, both cities with high Danish-American populations. Based on the 2000 U.S. Census, Omaha had the highest number of individuals claiming Danish ancestry when compared to all other cities.

Surrounding the museum is the Jens Jensen Prairie Landscape Park. The 30-acre park is named in honor of Danish immigrant Jens Jensen, a pioneer of the "prairie school" of landscape architecture and early advocate for using native plants in park and garden design. The park features a restored prairie ecosystem, walking trails, and design features like stone Council Rings that are frequently found in Jensen's designs.

Visitors to the museum can walk along the Little Mermaid Trail–a paved pedestrian path–to reach Bedstemor's House in the heart of Elk Horn. Built in 1908 and restored to that period, this immigrant home is listed on the National Register of Historic Places. There are two additional historical buildings on the museum grounds–a miniature chapel and a North Dakota homesteader's cabin. All are open to the public. The museum's Family History & Genealogy Center offers specialized resources for anyone tracing their family roots to Denmark. The reference library and research materials are available for visitors to use, and expert assistance is available from staff and volunteers. For those who can't visit Elk Horn in person, the Family History & Genealogy Center offers research and translation services. For more information about the museum's services, exhibitions, and current visiting hours, visit the museum's website: www.danishmuseum.org.

Most Popular Last Names on Wall of Honor

ANDERSEN, Hans & Bodil, Tyler, Minnesota

BERG, Jens Jim Christian Bjerg, Modesto, California

CHRISTENSEN, Chris & Valborg Sorensen, Omaha, Nebraska

DAMGAARD, Otto & Mary, Long Grove, Illinois

ESBECK, Niels Jensen & Mette Marie Poulsdatter, Guthrie County, Iowa

FABER, Frederik E., Chicago, Illinois

GODDIK, Lisbeth, Corvallis, Oregon

HANSEN, Johanne Maren, Grayling, Michigan

IVERSEN, Andreas, Sheffield, Illinois

JACOBSEN, Jacob Christian, Granly, Mississippi

JENSEN, Jens & Sophie, Sidney, Montana

KNUDSEN, Christen M. & Martha Madsen, Des Moines, Iowa

LARSEN, Christian B. & Abelone (Nielsen), Blair, Nebraska

MADSEN, Hans & Elise Marie Petersen, Omaha, Nebraska

MORTENSEN, Soren Hansen & Bodil Marie Maimburg, Lakewood, Ohio

NELSON, Jeppe, Harlan, Iowa

NIELSEN, Jorgen Skovgaard, Duxbury, Massachusetts

OLESEN, Nikolaj & Kirsten Solevad, Salinas, California

PEDERSEN, Magnus, Cuppy's Grove, Iowa

RASMUSSEN, Marie Elizabeth Duus, Askov, Minnesota

SORENSEN, Gerda Skov, Eugene, Oregon

THOMSEN, Thomas Vagn, Albany, New York

WIEGHORST, Olaf, El Cajon, California

A Heritage Tour

The sixty-foot-fall Danish Windmill catches your eye as your drive into town a few miles north of Interstate 80. The mill was found in Nørre Snede, Jutland, by Harvey Sornson. As a community project, the mill was purchased, dismantled, and shipped across the Atlantic. Its numbered pieces were reassembled in Elk Horn by volunteers. It now attracts more than 80,000 tourists a year. The flour it grinds is sold with other Danish delights in the adjacent gift shop. A bust of Hans Christian Andersen is on the grounds.

There are eighteen stops on the Danish Heritage Tour of Elk Horn and Kimballton. The houses at 4215 and 4227 Main Street are Danish-American classics, the proportions and central dormers reflect the style of the traditional Danish farm house.

The Salem Lutheran Retirement Home dates from the early 1960s, but once housed a Folk School, then a college preparatory school, a seminary, and Elk Horn College. It was rebuilt after a 1910 fire. Two buildings that escaped destruction in the 1910 fire were moved to serve as homes. Now at 4231 Union Street, *Gladhjem* (Happy Home) was once a dormitory and also the original publishing house for the weekly newspaper *Dannevirke*. The house at 2013 Washington Street was built in 1879 as a residence for Kristian Østergaard, the Folk School's teacher and hymn writer.

Near *Gladhjem* is a house that re-creates the atmosphere of immigrant homes between 1900 and 1910. Now called *Bedstemor's House,* it was built and lavishly decorated by a lovelorn immigrant, Otto Christensen, a man who stood so stiff and upright in his tailored coat and derby hat that the townspeople nicknamed him "Prince Otto." Christensen fell in love but spoke not a word of his feelings until he had completed the elaborate, two-story home. The lady of his dreams would have neither him nor the house. He could not bear to live in it without her, and from 1908 until the 1940s, he house was occupied by renters. It was then given to the Salem Lutheran Home to help pay for Christensen's nursing home expenses. Meta Mortensen bought the house in 1946 and lived in it for thirty-five years. In 1982, the house was purchased by the Elk Horn-Kimballton Arts Council, whose volunteers restored and furnished it. The Museum of Danish America now owns and operates the house, which is open to visitors.

Niels Steffensen, a blacksmith and farmer, built the cross-wing-style house at 2125 Park Street in 1885. Carl V. Andersen, a talented Danish carpenter, built the Victorian house at 2105 Pleasant Street in 1898.

The present Elk Horn Lutheran Church was built in 1948. A model ship hangs on the wall of the nave, an old Danish custom of petitioning for the safety of ships and seamen. The church also has a replica of Bertel Thorvaldsen's "Kristus" and an angel holding the baptismal font. The cemetery behind the church dates from 1876.

With the coming of the trains, goods could be shipped in and out with ease, and the people were in closer touch with the outside world. But west of Highway 173 between Elk Horn and Kimballton is a railroad cut—all that is left of the Atlantic Northern Railroad built in 1907.

Kimballton's Crystal Springs Creamery, a cooperative, sold $80,000 worth of milk in its first year in 1890. The immigrant buttermakers were the best in the business. The 1903 red block building was in use until 1992.

On the hillside west of the creamery, Crystal Springs Clay Products was established in 1908 to satisfy the desire for brick construction that reminded the Danes of home. Nels Bennedsen and others knew how to lay those bricks to perfection. Eventually the company became Roxy Clay Products, specializing in tiles to drain low-lying farmland. Kimballton's General Store Museum on Main Street displays Crystal Springs Clay products and information on the work of Bennedsen. Step inside and you're in a small-town general store of the early twentieth century.

Another Kimballton landmark is the *Forsamlingshus* (Assembly Hall) built in 1896. It served a church before a house of worship was built and also was the scene of dances, cultural events, plays, and gymnastic activities. When anyone suggested they might have built a church first, the people took comfort in the remark of a Minnesota Dane, "You can hold church services in a gym, but you can't hold gym in a church."

Immanuel Lutheran Church, Kimballton, which is on the National Register of Historic Places, was built in 1907 in a style typical of the wood frame Danish church in America. The nave is in the shape of a cross, and the altar, pulpit, lectern, and chandelier are all original. This church also has the ship model and a statue of Christ. The altar cloth is cutwork, a traditional handiwork style of many Danish-American women.

In the Kimballton park is a replica of Copenhagen's Little Mermaid. The park's benches invite you to sit and rest. The park's half-timbered *(bindingsvaerk)* cottage has a stork's nest on top.

Some of the stops on this tour are private and can be enjoyed only from the outside. Other sites are marked as "open." Step back in time and see what Danish Americans wrote home in their letters about this rich prairie.

Elk Horn and Kimballtown, Iowa

In the 1980s the crazy dream of Harvey Sornson of reconstructing an 1848 Danish Windmill in Elk Horn was in full swing. It took one year and 300 volunteers to rebuild and restore the now 165 year old mill back to life. The Danish Mill Corporation Board of Directors has recently taken on a project to further demonstrate its Danish heritage and entertain its many visitors. The construction of a Viking*Hjem* (Viking home) on the windmill's grounds will offer tourists a chance to really take a step back in time. The two structures, the Mill and the Viking*Hjem*, will complement one another through their historical significance. The Danish community of Elk Horn, Iowa offers tourists a taste of the Old World with no passport required. The town's Danish heritage is showcased by the 1800s authentic Danish Windmill. You can take a guided tour of the Windmill which starts with a 15 minute video, and then you can climb to the top and see the shuttered sails, grinding stones, and gearing made of wood and iron cogs. See how it all works together to grind wheat and rye flours with wind as the did 150 years ago.

The new Viking*Hjem* demonstrates a typical structure used throughout Scandinavia and Northern Europe during the latter Dark Ages to the early Middle Ages. You can experience the life of a Viking Smithy in A.D. 900 from the blacksmith shop and woodworking area to the demonstrations and lectures. We are excited that you will stop in Elk Horn to visit us!

Velkommen, 4038 Main Street, Elk Horn, Iowa

1-800-451-7960 www.danishwindmill.com

—Lisa Riggs, director, Danish Windmill and Viking*Hjem*

There is a replica of the Little Mermaid in Kimballtown, Iowa and in Solvang California. The year 2013 marks the 100th anniversary of the famous Little Mermaid statue in the Copenhagen Harbor in Denmark. The Little Mermaid *is a fairy tale by Hans Christian Andersen.*

Bedstemor House in Elk Horn, Iowa
Left above top: *Historic items in the collection of the Danish Museum of America*
Left below: *Grindstone, Danish Windmill, Elk Horn, Iowa*

Drawings by Diane Heusinkveld

Grand Goals at Grand View University

Grand View University in Des Moines, Iowa, is rooted in the Danish Evangelical Lutheran Church in America, whose 1893 convention in Racine, Wisconsin, launched plans for a seminary. A year later, the plans called for creation of "the Danish Lutheran Church's University."

Bids came from Chicago and from Atlantic, Sioux City, and Des Moines in Iowa. Pastor O.L. Kirkeberg, leader of the Elk Horn Folk School, endorsed Des Moines and carried the day. The location is slightly less than two miles north of the Iowa State Capitol.

A former pastor, D.H. Kooker, later a real estate developer and banker in Des Moines, donated one block in the Grand View addition and the option to buy or find purchasers for 100 additional lots by 1895. Kooker also promised to provide 60,000 bricks for the school's foundation with the understanding that the structure would be ready for use by the end of 1895.

Fund-raising literature of the day read, "The free-born Danish spirit craves a home for the freedom of the spirit; a home from whose gables shall wave the banner of spiritual freedom and from whose windows the view shall be clear and unhampered in all directions."

The college was welcomed by the 238 Des Moines citizens of Danish birth, especially a few who were extremely vocal, were tired of being mistaken for Swedes, and wanted it known that they had a culture of their own.

The first phase of the building was finished in 1895. Gables were designed in the Danish Renaissance style made popular by King Christian IV in the early seventeenth century. The school opened in the fall of 1896 with one student, Nils Jul Mikkelsen.

Around the turn of the century, the cost for room, board, and tuition was around $14 for four weeks—$15 in the winter.

In the 1902–03 school year, the eighty-seven students included forty from Denmark and forty-seven from Danish-American families. During the early years, the Danish language was the principal means of communication and instruction. As late as 1941, reports to the synod convention were printed in Danish. The language of the homeland was no longer used in classes after World War I. It persisted into the thirties in the Seminary. The Seminary became a part of the Lutheran School of Theology, moving to Chicago in 1960.

Rapid expansion beginning in the 1960s included in a new gymnasium, a men's residence hall, the science-classroom building, a new women's residence hall, the college library, and College Center. The Cowles Communication Center is a state-of-the-art laboratory for journalism students. The student newspaper is *Grand Views.*

Grand View University is described as "in independent, four-year liberal arts co-educational college affiliated with the Evangelical Lutheran Church in America."

Grand View University offers forty undergraduate majors and twenty-nine minors, as well as many pre-professional and certificate programs. They also offer several graduate track programs in nursing, business, and education. Enrollment is under 2,500, which offers students the opportunity for individual attention from faculty members, with a fourteen to one faculty-to-student ratio. The campus has all the cultural advantages of being within a city. More than seventy-two percent of all the students receive financial aid, and the tuition is the lowest of any of the four-year independent colleges in Iowa.

The *Studenterfest,* Grand View's homecoming, continues the college tradition of dramatic presentations. An important part of *Studenterfest* in the early years was folk dancing and, while interest in this activity has waned, it still survives.

In 1932, the first layman president (also the first American born), C. Arild Olsen, was installed at Grand View. Kent Henning became the thirteenth president in 2000.

Danishness can still be seen and felt on the Grand View campus, from the heraldic lions, the hearts, and the step-gabled church depicted on a stained glass window to the crimson robes of the Grand View Choir and the red and white uniforms of the athletes proudly known as the Grand View Vikings. The college offers a minor in Scandinavian Studies.

Grand View makes the promise, "You won't graduate with just a head of unrelated facts. You will have the ability to analyze situations, solve problems, and think creatively."

Old World Wisconsin

Old World Wisconsin, the outdoor living history museum in Kettle Moraine State Forest near Eagle, Wisconsin, provides a vivid re-creation of life for the newly arrived European immigrants who settled the upper midwest in the late 19th century. More than 60 structures were thoroughly researched, then dismantled (each board numbered), moved to the museum site and painstakingly reassembled precisely as they had originally been constructed. The collection stands as the largest museum in the world dedicated to the history of rural life.

Kristen Pedersen's 1890 log farmhouse, from Polk County in northwest Wisconsin reflects the Danish lifestyle. Pederen was a native of Langskov, Denmark. Twice married, he tragically lost both wives to child-birth related complications. No doubt, the *ableskiver* recipe contributed by the Old World Wisconsin museum (found on page 147) would have been a very special treat for a man such as Pedersen.

The Kristen Pedersen farmhouse, Old World Wisconsin

Skovsøen (Lake of the Woods)

Concordia Language Villages, a program of Concordia College in Moorhead, Minnesota, sponsors a summer program where young people choose one of fifteen language Villages and "live" in the language and culture together with others of their age. Languages taught are Arabic, Chinese, Danish, Finnish, French, German, Japanese, Korean, Norwegian, Portuguese, Russian, Spanish, and Swedish. The Norwegian, German, French, Russian, Swedish, Spanish, and Finnish Villages are culturally authentic year-round sites on Turtle River Lake, near Bemidji, Minnesota. The beautiful lakeside facilities are leased for others, including Danish. Each permanent Village features architecturally authentic buildings on a campus, which includes sleeping facilities and an activity/dining hall, a village store, bank, and post office. "Passports" are issued by the Language Village office.

The Danish Language Village is *Skovsøen,* which means "lake of the woods." Arriving participants are met by the *told* (customs officials), who inspect their luggage and stamp their passports as if they were coming into Kastrup Lufthavn in København (Kastrup Airport in Copenhagen.) Their money is changed into Danish kroner, and they choose Danish names to be used during their stay.

Days begin with *Fiskeklubben* for those who want to try their luck at a well-stocked trout lake, or *Vikingklubben* for the hearty types who prefer a swim and sauna before breakfast.

The whole Village turns out soon after the wake-up bell for *flagheising* (raising the *Dannebrog,* or Danish flag) and *morgensang* (breakfast-time group singing).

Informal Danish instruction is constant, large and small group language sessions to expand the vocabulary. Sports and crafts are offered, and the bank is open for withdrawing *kroner* to spend at the *butik* (store). The food is traditional Danish fare called by the proper Danish names.

Nature hikes, water sports, singing, *folkedans* (folk dancing), and meetings of special interest groups fill the afternoons, and then it's time for a bountiful Danish dinner.

After the evening meal, the whole Village participates in a variety of evening programs. Among them are a simulation of a Faeroe Islands whaling expedition, a dance celebration of Midsommer, and a carnival-like Tivoli party. Each program often culminates with a bonfire, singing, and the roasting of *snobrød.*

Sometime during the summer, a day is set aside to celebrate a real Dansk Jul with woven hearts, Christmas carols, a gift exchange, an authentic Danish Christmas dinner, and a dance around the Christmas tree in the woods.

The staff at Skovsøen includes native Danes and also Americans who have lived in Denmark or studied the language and culture. The sessions are one or two weeks for seven- to eighteen-year-olds at all levels of instruction. Four-week summer programs are offered for high school credit for grades nine through twelve. Students can earn a full year of language credit in one month.

Even the short-term sessions get impressive results. One parent wrote: "You taught them more Danish in two weeks than I have in all their lives."

The low cost includes tuition, food, lodging, insurance, instruction, and instructional materials.

For more information, visit: www.concordialanguagevillages.org and click on the "Danish" tab.

Photo courtesy Concordia Language Villages

Cultural authenticity is an important factor in retaining the immersion simulation at Skovsøen and is expressed in all activities, including song and dance. Singing around the camp fire—students are singing our Skovsøen theme song!

Skovsøen is the Danish language and culture program of Concordia Language Villages, located in Bemidji, Minnesota. Handicrafts outside—this young woman is making her own purse.

Photos courtesy Concordia Language Villages

Teenagers make traditional æbleskiver over the camp fire—they eat them with powdered sugar and jelly! Culturally authentic cuisine is an important factor in the complete immersion simulation at Skovsøen, the Danish Language Village.

Danebod
Fellowship in Minnesota

Echoes of the folk-school ideal linger. At Tyler, Minnesota, the Danebod Danish Folk Meeting dropped the word "Danish" several years ago and is now simply the Danebod Folk Meeting, but there is a traditional Danish service on Sunday morning, and two daily singing periods involve Danish songs and songs in English.

The Folk Meeting starts with supper on a Wednesday and ends with dinner Sunday noon. There are morning, afternoon, and evening lectures on a wide variety of topics; morning and evening devotions; a daily story period; and folk dancing after the evening coffee. The emphasis is on education, inspiration, and fellowship, following in the footsteps of the Danish-American folk schools.

Participants come from the East and West Coasts and points between. Speakers have included Walter Capps of the University of California at Santa Barbara; James A. Nestingen of Luther Northwestern Theological Seminary in St. Paul; June Sampson, director of the Museum of Danish America at Elk Horn, Iowa; and Pastors Lars and Bodil Toftdahl of Calgary, Alberta, Canada. Some bring their own bedding and stay at the folk school, while others stay at motels. Electric hookups are available for campers, and some people bring recreational vehicles or tents. Meetings are in late August, and reservations are made as early as May. Danebod also hosts a popular series of summer family recreation camps.

Young people under college age must be accompanied by a parent or chaperon, and, although children are the responsibility of their parents, babysitters are on duty after 8 p.m.

Crafts offered include: model airplanes, woodworking, smocking, weaving, computers, haiku, folk arts, basket weaving, rockets and launchers, mixed media in art, *scherenschnitte* (paper cutting), stained glass, calligraphy, lap quilting, silk screen printing, mounting and matting, origami, photography, and children's crafts.

Solvang: Denmark in California

In Southern California there is a little "Old World" town founded by ⌐.
and popular with visitors in all seasons. This is Solvang, north of Santa Barbara via Routes 154 and 24.

Here are *bindingsvaerk* (timber-framed crossbeam design), thatched roofs with wooden storks, and flashes of green copper. Solvang's Bethania Lutheran Church is modeled after Bishop Grundtvig's step-gabled church in Copenhagen. The rigged ship model that hangs from the ceiling in the center of the sanctuary is a replica of Bartal Thorvaldsen's famous sculpture.

During the Danish Lutheran Church Convention of June 1910, it was decided to found a Danish colony on the West Coast. Its focus was to be a Danish folk school, a school for life that would preserve the Danish heritage.

Rev. J.M. Gregersen, Rev. Benedict Nordentoft, and Professor P.P. Hornsyld made a prospecting expedition to California and chose this fresh, high valley site between the Santa Ynez and San Rafael Mountains. They purchased more than 9,000 acres and named it Solvang, which means "sunny field."

Atterdag College was founded in 1911 and operated until 1937 when it succumbed to the Great Depression. Gary and Kathy Mullins of Solvang, owners of The Book Loft, hope that a scale model of Atterdag, which they commissioned, will generate support for restoring Danish culture programs of the college and even a Danish folk school. After all, *Atterdag* means "there shall be another day."

Ferdinand Sorensen, who came to Solvang in 1933, is the father of Danish architecture in Solvang. He carved the storks and used the Danish provincial architecture in building his own house, *Møllebakken,* and Solvang's first provincial-style windmill, the Mill on the Hill. On a two-ton rock barrow (a reproduction of a burial mound of the early Vikings), he inscribed the message "11,270 Km to Solvang."

Characters from Hans Christian Andersen's fairy tales shared the rooftops with storks and *nisser* (elf-like creatures), and the arms of Danish windmills turn in the breeze. Rasmussen's Gift Store is typical of the Danish provincial buildings. The thatched roofs are actually made of jagged wooden shingles, and blue-green roofs of aged copper. The storks bring good luck. Solvang was a romantic spot for actress Rosalind Russell, who chose it as the setting for her marriage to Freddie Brisson, a Dane.

It's Christmas all year long in Solvang, with shops displaying Danish Christmas ornaments and toys, including dolls in authentic Danish dress. You can find everything from amber paperweights to giant *Bosendørfer* grand pianos. The Danish shopping complex, Tivoli Square, has it all, and the clock tower in the center of the square houses four bronze bells that strike for hours. The Chimney Sweep Inn has cottages named for characters in the fantasies of C. S. Lewis.

If it's mealtime, you'll find the best, from sweets at a sidewalk café to the endless offerings of a smorgasbord, and there are also restaurants with ethnic cooking other than Danish.

Among the monuments are a bust of Hans Christian Andersen and a replica of the Ericksen bronze of the Little Mermaid in Copenhagen's harbor.

Folk singers, groups of roving singers, and Danish folk dancers perform frequently. They're a colorful sight with the Hamlet Square "Blue Windmill" as a backdrop. The popular "Danish Days" celebration is traditionally the third weekend in September.

Solvang, California   *Photo Solvang USA.com*

Diane Heusinkveld

Rasmussen's Solvang was founded in 1921 by Dannish immigrants who first settled in Hampton, Iowa and then moved to Solvang, site of a Danish colony. The store today, featuring Scandinavian books and gifts is owned by David Rassmussen, a third generation Danish American.

The Danish Sisterhood of America

The Danish Sisterhood of America was born on December 15, 1883, with the founding of the Christine Lodge #1 in Negaunee, Michigan. Lodge #2 was at Lyons, Iowa, followed on March 20, 1884, and Lodge #3 at Davenport, Iowa, dates from September 14, 1884. The Supreme Lodge was chartered in Illinois in 1891.

Of the 179 lodges formed for the dual purpose of funeral benefits and preservation of Danish traditions and culture, forty-eight remain.

There is one lodge outside the United States in Vancouver, B.C., Canada.

Women from eighteen to fifty-nine who are of Danish birth, descent, or heritage or who are married to men of such qualifications are eligible for membership.

The Junior American Danish Auxiliary (JADA) for young people under sixteen preserves the Danish heritage by teaching the language, dances, and crafts.

Every Day is Flag Day

Invited to visit at a home, a guest in Denmark may be surprised to see the Danish flag flying in his or her honor at the home. Every home has a flag, and Danes fly it on special occasions, such as birthdays, baptisms, anniversaries, graduations, and weddings, as well as on official holidays. Danes use small flags to decorate the Christmas tree and the dining room table. When the framework of a new building is completed, a little fir tree and flags are placed on the top. One of my earliest memories is waking up on the morning of my birthday to discover at my bedside a table covered with an embroidered tablecloth, a bouquet of roses, and prettily wrapped presents, flanked by a Danish flag and an American flag on miniature brass flag poles. Every day is flag day in Denmark.

—Ingrid Marie Christiansen

The Old Man of the Mountain

"Tomorrow is strangely the enemy of today, as today has already forgotten yesterday." —Gutzon Borglum

The Mount Rushmore National Memorial, about twenty-five miles southwest of Rapid City, is well within the seemingly endless Black Hills, so named by the Native Americans for pine forests so vast that they darkened the ground beneath. The Memorial, with its sculpted heads of four American presidents—George Washington, Thomas Jefferson, Abraham Lincoln, and Theodore Roosevelt—suggest the nation's founding, its philosophy of freedom, the preservation of the Union, and the importance of conservation and national parks. Each of the heads measures at least sixty feet from hair to chin, but appears much smaller, of course, when viewed from the ground.

Almost stealing the scene from the Memorial's four great presidents is its colorful sculptor, who started work in 1927 and in the next fourteen years managed about six and a half years of actual working time, as weather and funds permitted, to create the masterpiece of his career, for which he earned less than $90,000.

Gutzon Borglum, the sculptor, was called "the old man" by work crews on the mountain, but never within his hearing. This volatile artists was by nature a dramatist and a romantic who viewed his own life story as a novel that could be revised, edited, and embellished. For instance, he changed his admitted birth date from 1867 to 1871 because he didn't feel as old as he was. He also "changed" mothers, and therein lies a tale.

The Borglums had a distinguished lineage, descending from the family de la Mothe. The name originated in 1189 when a medieval knight named Conrad Reinhardt went to the Holy Land with the Holy Roman emperor Frederick I Barbarossa of Germany to recapture Jerusalem on the Third Crusade. Reinhardt saved the emperor from being attacked by a wild boar (some say it was a billy goat), and Barbarossa gave him a title, "de la Mothe," meaning the one of courage. In the following century, some Reinhardt descendents settled in the north of Denmark. The family took Borglum, the name of the place, as its own.

Borglum's father, Jens Moller Hangard Borglum, was a wood carver. Converted by Mormon missionaries, he set out for the "New Zion" in America. Among the new Mormons aboard the ship, he met Ida Mikkelsen, daughter of a Copenhagen furrier, and they were married. They made their way from New York to Nebraska City, where they joined a Mormon wagon train. They had no money for oxen and a wagon, so they bought a wheeled pushcart and walked the 900 miles to Utah. Later, Ida's younger sister Christina joined them. Jens took the eighteen-year-old Christina as his second wife as permitted by Mormon tradition. John Gutzon de la Mothe Borglum was born in Ovid, Idaho, to Jens Borglum and Christina. Christina opted out of the marriage two years later, leaving her two sons, Gutzon and Solon, with her sister Ida and their father. In claiming Ida as his mother, Gutzon was choosing the woman who nurtured him from such an early age.

Gutzon Borglum encountered the impossible dream as a small boy. The full moon rose, and he wanted to get his hands on it. Jumping down from his father's carriage, he ran toward the moonlight, reaching. But the moon itself eluded him, and when he realized he could not grasp it, he wept.

Borglum studied art and painting in California. Winning a commission to paint a portrait of General John Charles Fremont, the great explorer of the West, he created such a fine likeness that he gained the lifelong support of the general's wife, Jessie Benton Fremont, who helped advance his career.

Borglum then studied with Elizabeth "Liza" Jaynes Putnam, an artist from a prominent Massachusetts family, and despite the difference in their ages (she was forty and he was twenty-two), they married in 1889 and she took him to Paris, where his interest in sculpture first stirred. He became a student and friend of Auguste Rodin, the sculptor. Later, the couple went to London, where Borglum opened a studio and was invited to display his paintings for Queen Victoria. He was moody and restless in London, so Liza took him back to Paris. Borglum went back to America alone, meeting his fate on the voyage in the form of Mary Montgomery, who had just earned her doctorate at the University of Berlin. In the summer of 1902, when Borglum had both a nervous breakdown and a near-fatal case of typhoid, both Liza and Mary rushed to his side. Liza later departed and Mary became his wife.

Borglum thought American art, like that of ancient Egypt, should be massive and soul-stirring, on a scale with the leaders whose life it expressed. "My big mission in life," he said, "is to get people to look at art in a big way and get away from petty stuff."

Borglum's concept for a monument at Stone Mountain, Georgia, was not fulfilled, but he earned practical experience in mountain art, and attracted the attention of Doane Robinson, South Dakota state historian, who first proposed the Black Hills project and wanted images of Chief Red Cloud of the Sioux, Lewis and Clark, and others of the West. Borglum visited Robinson several times, once staying two weeks checking potential mountain sites. It was Borglum who insisted on a national, rather than a regional, monument. In 1925, both the United States Congress and the South Dakota Legislature voted approval of the idea.

President Calvin Coolidge visited the project in 1927, giving Borglum six steel drills to begin carving that day. Borglum was lowered by cable onto the face of the cliff and made the first cuts for the face of Washington. Congress voted $250,000 in 1929, and by 1938 had nearly a million dollars in the project, which has been more than repaid in government fees and earnings at the site.

At one time when money was scarce, someone asked Borglum about the great expense of the monument, and he said, "Call up Cheops and ask how much his pyramid in Egypt cost and what he paid the creator. It was inferior work to Mount Rushmore."

In 1940, Congress voted an annual appropriation to complete the sculpture.

Neither Borglum nor his "Shrine of Democracy" escaped controversy. A 1992 article in the *Smithsonian* magazine included such terms as irreverent, bizarre, preposterous, outrageous, overstatement, politicians, and

Mount Rushmore National Memorial
Black Hills of South Dakota

From left: *George Washington, Thomas Jefferson, Theodore Roosevelt, and Abraham Lincoln*

"wilderness...miles from everywhere." The writer described Borglum as hot-eyed, densely mustached, intractable, feisty, feuding, and tempestuous. Still, bizarre opinions aside, the Mount Rushmore National Memorial attracts into this beautiful "wilderness" more than two million visitors a year.

Borglum died in a Chicago hospital after an operation March 6, 1941, leaving unfinished Roosevelt's features, the hair of Jefferson, Roosevelt, and Lincoln, and the lapels and collar of Washington. Borglum's son Lincoln took over, and the work was finished October 31, 1941.

Gutzon Borglum was buried in Forest Lawn Cemetery, Glendale, California, among the famous dead. With the creation of the Mount Rushmore National Memorial, he finally caught the moon, in a manner of speaking. Badger Clark, the poet laureate of South Dakota, eulogized Borglum, saying, "Coming generations 5,000 years hence will not ask who the characters on the mountain are, but who carved them." The old-timers on the project said, "He was somebody you could ride the river with."

Thorvaldsen's "Kristus"

Danish-American churches that are fortunate enough to have reproductions of "Kristus," Bertel Thorvaldsen's famous statue of Christ, are taking good care of these treasures because they cannot be replaced. The only copies now being made are just six inches tall. The original figure of Christ with arms outstretched to humanity was completed in Rome in 1821 and is now in *Vor Fruekirke* (Church of Our Lady) in Copenhagen.

The sculptor worked on the piece for two years. Legend has it that he was not satisfied with the clay figure when he left his studio one night. In the morning, he was shocked to see the clay had settled, moving the arms forward and opening the hands. The Thorvaldsen Museum in Copenhagen explains the creation less miraculously: In 1819, Thorvaldsen felt driven to produce a likeness of Christ different from all others. He rejected the theatrical look of the Dennecker Christ, which seemed to say "Through me to the Father." Neither did he want the pained, languishing Christ seen in Catholic churches, with eyes fixed on heaven. He wanted a Christ noble in a simplicity that would not become dated. After all, he said, "Christ stands over millennia."

One day in June 1821, he modeled a Christ with arms reaching up to heaven. He stood looking at the figure when a friend arrived. The friend stood in front of the model, crossing his arms, and the sculptor was moved to turn the upraised arms downward, expressing the divine invitation.

"So now I have it!" said Thorvaldsen. "So it shall be!"

And so it has been in churches all over the United States. Early in the twentieth century, a mold for Thorvaldsen's "Kristus" was used for figures "in a size suitable for churches," and many of those Christ figures have brown hair, blue eyes, and pale-colored face, hands, and feet. The coloring began with an 1887 experiment by Bing & Grøndahl that defied Thorvaldsen's artistic intentions but pleased many patrons.

The Happy Danes, The Holy Danes

Although I grew up in a home that seemed as Danish-American as any, I was well into adulthood before I heard about the "Happy Danes" and the "Holy Danes." I was at a state convention of the Danish Sisterhood of America when the subject came up, and my ignorance of the designations was cause for amazement and mirth. I thought they were talking about drinkers and teetotalers, but obviously they weren't.

I wondered: Where did my family fit? We were happy on occasion and did our best to be holy when that condition was appropriate. Did you have to be one or the other?

Eventually, I discovered that the Happy Danes were followers of Nikolai Frederik Severin Grundtvig (1783–1872), who conceived the folk high schools and was the founder of adult education in Denmark as well as among the Danish immigrants in America.

The Holy Danes were the pietists of the Inner Mission group. They scorned the secular emphasis of the Grundtvigianers and insisted that their efforts to retain the Danish language and culture in America held back their children's progress in the new land.

The differences between these factions split the Danish Lutheran Church in America in 1894 and produced the Danish Evangelical Lutheran Church in North America (the Happy Danes) and the United Danish Lutheran Church in America (the Holy Danes). At first, the Holy Danes outnumbered the Happy Danes, but the Happy faction were the most vocal. Today, both these groups are a part of the Evangelical Lutheran Church in America, and scarcely anyone would take the trouble to sort out the Happies and the Holies. If they did, they'd probably find some of each on both sides of the fence. And drinking has nothing to do with it.

Danish Needlework

Under the patronage of Her Majesty the Queen of Denmark, instructive books on the traditional arts have been published.

Available in English, *Danish Floral Charted Designs* by Gerda Bengstssen includes Lapland rhododendron, and ladies mantle patterns for a variety of projects from decorating small pillows to large bedspreads. The author is a noted designer of counted cross-stitch. Her designs were originally created for counted cross-stitch, but may be used in many other forms of needlework such as needlepoint, latch-hook, crocheting, and knitting. Another title available in English is *Danish Pulled Thread Embroidery,* by Esther Fangel, Ida Winckler, and Agnete Wuldern Madsen, produced by the Danish Handworkers Guild in Danish and in English. Prized for hundreds of years in Denmark, this embroidery is used for making doilies, table mats and tablecloths, and decoration of clothing requiring a delicate touch. Both titles are from Dover Publications, Inc.

Artifacts from the Viking Age clearly indicate that Danish women loved embroidery and created decorative collars centuries ago. In 1928, the Danish society *Haandarbejdets Fremme* (Danish Design) was founded to revive embroidery and home industries.

Danish Lace Designs

The Legend of Queen Dagmar

The story of Queen Dagmar, wife of thirteenth-century ruler Valdemar the Victorious, became a lasting legend. Dagmar (softly pronounced as "Dowmer" with the accent on the first syllable) was a beautiful Bohemian princess known as the Sunrise Maiden because her name meant "Dawn." Early in the eighteenth century Dagmar's grave in Ringsted was cleared, and diggers unearthed a gold and enamel cross which the queen had always worn. The crucified Christ was on one side, Christ and the four gospels were on the other side. The Dagmar Cross became the traditional christening gift for Danish girls.

Valdemar's next wife was the Portuguese princess Berengaria, changed to Berngard, which in Danish means "the bear's keeper." She was, by all accounts, a beautiful but evil woman who wanted to reserve for herself alone the right to wear red. Danish women rose up in wrath, and the edict was never issued. The red so beloved of the Danes combines with white in the *Dannebrog*, the national flag. A legend holds that the original "Danes' piece of cloth" floated down from heaven during the battle of Lyndanisse that won Estonia for the Danes in 1219.

Greenland

Greenland, the largest island in the world, appropriately is allied with Denmark, which has been called the nation of 400 islands. Also appropriate is that the uninhabited Greenland National Park—the northeast third of the island—is the largest park in the world. This island of the far north was named by Eric the Red, who discovered it about A.D. 960, and hoped the name would attract settlers. Green it may be along the southwest shoreline, but the vast interior—more than three-fourths of it north of the Arctic Circle—is snow, ice sheets, and polar bears. Greenland ice can be a mile deep; the thickest is about 9,000 feet. The total ice mass is second only to that of Antarctica. The island is about 1,660 miles long and 750 miles wide, with the ice sheet covering more than eighty percent of the land. The nearest land to the west is Canada, and to the east is Iceland. Greenland's north shore is within 500 miles of the North Pole.

The glaciers of Greenland grind slowly as gravity pulls them toward the sea, to which they contribute icebergs that float south toward major shipping lanes. On April 15, 1912, a huge iceberg had drifted to a point about 1,600 miles northeast of New York City, where it was struck by the 46,000-ton Titanic, traveling at full speed on its maiden voyage from England to New

York. The Titanic, the world's largest ship at the time, sank. More than 2,200 were aboard, and more than 1,500 perished.

In the years following the discovery of Greenland, about 3,000 Norwegians and Icelanders lived there. They engaged in farming, severely limited by the cold, and fishing. Their numbers were dwindling by 1397, when Greenland became Denmark's as a result of the Kalmar Union (1397–1523), during which Denmark, Norway, and Sweden were under the same monarch. The recolonizing dates from 1721, when Hans Egede, a Danish-Norwegian clergyman, established a trading company and Lutheran mission in Greenland. Today, about 57,000 people call Greenland home, including 10,000 Danes. The Ancestry of the Greenlanders is Innuit (Eskimo), European, or both. All Greenlanders have full rights of Danish citizenship. The most populous region is still the southwest shore. Fishing—eighty percent shrimp—is the largest industry. Some grains are grown during the short summers, and, as permitted by climate, sheep, cattle, reindeer, and poultry are raised. Cars are used in towns, but travel to other communities is by boat or by chartered planes. In the north the Innuit use sled dogs. Greenland is treeless; all lumber for homes and other buildings is imported.

Greenland's southernmost cities are Julianehaab and Ivigtut. Others include Godthaab (which is the capital and has a college), Godhavn, Upernavik, Dundas, and Thule, which was founded in 1910 by the Danish explorer Knud Rasmussen, and several settlements on the east shore. Cryolite, which is used in aluminum, was mined for nearly a century at Ivigtut.

All children age seven to fourteen attend schools. The Greenlandic and Danish languages are used, and many textbooks are printed in Greenland.

The Greenlanders adopted a new constitution in 1953, and have been self-governing since 1978, electing the twenty-seven members of the *Landsting*, the legislative body. Greenlanders elect two members of the Danish *Folketing*, the national assembly. When the United States entered World War II, it undertook protection of Greenland at Danish request. Today in Greenland the United States operates Thule Air Force Base, a radar warning system, and weather stations. Tunneled into ice, one of these stations has atomic power.

And, of course, what would Greenland and the North Pole be without Santa Claus? When the number of letters to Santa Claus increased to 80,000 in one year, Santa Claus opened his own "Santa's Post Office" in Nuuk, Greenland. Each letter is answered. Santa Claus, who lives in a snow castle close to the North Pole, also produces Christmas gifts all year at Santa's Workshop in Nuuk on the Colonial Harbor, close to the gift shop and Café Rudolph.

There are many flights each week between Copenhagen and Greenland, and several flights from the United States to Greenland and the Faeroe Islands.

The Far-Away Faeroes

The Faeroe Islands in the North Atlantic are a semi-autonomous province of Denmark. Eighteen of the islands, totaling about 540 square miles, are inhabited. The nearest lands are Iceland, 250 miles northwest, and the Scottish Shetlands, 200 miles southeast. Their thick layers of basilica lava tilt southeast. During the last Ice Age, intense glaciation gouged fault valleys into deep U-shaped troughs, called fjords. The highest elevations are along the great sea cliffs of the northwest. The highest peak, Slaettaratindur, rises 2,894 feet. The total population of the islands numbers about 48,800.

The islands were first settled by Irish monks about A.D. 700 and were occupied by Vikings in the early ninth century. About A.D. 1000, the King of Norway ordered the people to become Christians. Remains of a thirteenth-century Gothic cathedral that was never completed may be seen at Kirkebø. Today, most islanders are Lutherans, members of the State Church.

The Faeroes became a Norwegian province in 1035 and, with Norway, came under Danish control in 1380 as a result of a marriage between the royal families of Denmark and Norway.

Most of the population perished in the Black Death epidemic of the mid-fourteenth century. Resettlement by western Norwegians took place during the sixteenth century.

Like the Icelandic language, the Faeroese language derives from the Old Norse dialect. It was put into written form in the nineteenth century in a drive for nationalism that brought about the restoration of the Faeroese *lagting,* or parliament, in 1852, and in 1856 ended the Danish royal trade monopoly that had been in effect since 1709.

During World War II, Great Britain controlled the Faeroes, keeping them out of German hands. After the war, in 1948, the island peoples received a large measure of autonomy and have their own flag, currency, and language. They also have two representatives in the *Folketing,* the Danish unicameral legislature. A commission represents the Danish Crown in the islands.

Sheep are the mainstay of earning a living. The name of the islands derives from old Norse words for "sheep islands." Fishing is also important. The chief export is dried cod. Spinning and knitting industries contribute to the economy. The Faeroese hunt puffins for food, and eider for down and feathers.

The Virgin Islands

Although Denmark sold its Virgin Islands to the United States in 1917, the Danish influence can still be seen in place names and architecture. In 1870, the United States Senate had refused to pay $7,500,00 for St. Thomas and St. John, but the U.S. aggressively sought the islands in World War I to control a major route to the Panama Canal. The price was $25 million in gold.

On his second voyage to the New World in 1493, Columbus landed at St. Croix and sighted St. Thomas and St. John, naming the island group for the legend of St. Ursula and the virgins who were massacred by the Huns of Cologne. Over the centuries that story grew until it told of 11,000 virgins massacred, and in the twentieth century, St. Ursula's feast day was dropped from the church calendar because of doubts as to the authenticity of the tale.

St. Croix, with eighty-four square miles of land, is the largest island. It is entirely in the Caribbean Sea. St. Thomas (thirty-two square miles) and St. John (twenty square miles) are about forty miles to the north, between the Atlantic and the Caribbean. The thirty-six British Virgin Islands are to the east; sixteen of them are inhabited. Columbus was chased away from St. Croix by the native population.

The islands once were strongholds of pirates. Danish settlement began in 1666. The Danes claimed St. John and other nearby islands in 1684, and purchased St. Croix in 1733 from France, which had controlled it since 1651.

Sugar cane and cotton trading were lucrative on St. Croix until the demand for both waned in the 1800s. Raising sugar cane was difficult without slave labor, but in 1792 Denmark became the first country in the world to ban slave-trading, and in 1848, Governor General Peter von Scholten granted freedom to the slaves of St. Thomas. This enlightened act occurred seventeen years before the freeing of the slaves in the United States, and it caused an immediate decline in the island's economy. Many descendants of the early slaves became Lutherans, and after 1917, some of them emigrated and became the core of a Black Lutheran congregation at Mount Olivet Church in Washington, D.C. As late as the 1950s, black Virgin Islanders were speaking Danish in Washington.

Charlotte Amalie on St. Thomas is the territorial capital of the United States Virgin Islands. Declared a free port in the mid-1700s, it became the third largest city in the Danish empire, one of the world's busiest ports, and,

Touches of Denmark in St. Thomas, Virgin Islands

by 1800, the trading center of the West Indies. Today, St. Thomas attracts to its lovely harbor more than 1,000 cruise ships annually. Charlotte Amalie is also home to the St. Thomas Synagogue, the second-oldest synagogue in the Western Hemisphere. Another lovely spot is Magens Bay, rated by *National Geographic* as one of the ten most beautiful beaches in the world.

St. John Island is now an unspoiled paradise maintained by the National Park Service. Here, as elsewhere in the islands, the aquamarine waters, tawny sand, and tropical greenery have all the allure that first attracted the Europeans to the islands.

Markers in an old cemetery on St. Thomas tell of shipwrecks, hurricanes, and yellow fever. Sailors and missionaries, soldiers, traders, politicians, and others rest side by side in a cemetery shared by Danes, Germans, French, Scots, Swedes, and English.

St. Croix has been ruled by seven nations, but Denmark controlled it longest, naming the principal cities Frederiksted and Christiansted in honor of Danish kings. On this island are the ruins of a Danish settlement.

Tourism is the principal industry of the islands. Visitors come from all over the world to enjoy the azure seas, the marine life, the beaches, the bargain shopping, and the rum. Visiting these idyllic islands, particularly in the dead of winter, makes it clear why the seventeenth-century Danes came and stayed. Although some 400 green islands surround the Danish mainland, they're not where the trade winds blow.

Seeing Denmark

Copenhagen is Europe's most laid-back capital. The motto there is *bare rolig,* which means "take it easy." Copenhagen is laced with canals on which you can take a sightseeing trip by boat. On a schooner trip into the Sound you can have lunch or dinner and see Copenhagen and the Little Mermaid. In Copenhagen you can go to the circus, the zoo, the wonderful aquarium, the beautiful Tycho Brahe Planetarium, and more. The Royal Theatre, more than 250 years old, offers plays, grand opera, operettas, and ballet. Three orchestras perform weekly at Radio Concert Hall. The Zealand Symphony gives more than 150 concerts in the summer, and jazz is heard in night clubs and bars, where food is served until dawn. Amalienborg Palace is the home of the Queen. The changing of the guard occurs at noon daily.

Museums and art galleries are numerous. The uncharacteristic Gauguins were painted while he briefly endured his Danish wife's homeland. Copenhagen's mile-long "walking street," the Strøget, is the shopper's paradise. And in Copenhagen and all of Denmark there are more than 850 castles, manor houses, and estates.

Tivoli, in the heart of Copenhagen, is the grandmother of all amusement parks. It was founded in 1843. A visitor in its first year was Hans Christian Andersen. Tivoli was the inspiration for his Chinese tale *The Nightingale.* An estimated 272 million people visited Tivoli in its first 150 years. In a nation of five million, four million visited Tivoli in 1992, about forty percent of them from countries other than Denmark. Tivoli's gardens boast nearly a half-million flowers. The park is famed for its eating places, its stage presentations, its music (from rock to waltz to classical), and most of all for its fun. On its outdoor stage, strong men and bearded ladies once entertained. In recent times, visitors have watched Marlene Dietrich, Joan Baez, Cher, Josephine Baker, Maurice Chevalier, Louis Armstrong, Duke Ellington, the Alvin Ailey American Dance Theater, the Manhattan Transfer, and others. Visiting Tivoli twice in the 1950s was Walt Disney, who came away with ideas for his theme parks in California and Florida.

The language barrier is non-existent in Denmark as most Danes speak Danish and English, and one or two other languages.

Restaurants serve salmon from the Baltic, ham from Danish porkers, open-face sandwiches, crisp vegetables from the fertile gardens of Denmark, pastries with the lightness borrowed from the Viennese, and sauces inspired by the French. Toast your holiday with Tuborg or Carlsberg beer or Danish aquavit. And there's never a shortage of coffee served in lovely blue and white cups.

For a small charge, the Copenhagen Card can be obtained from railroad stations, hotels, and travel agencies. In and near Copenhagen, it is a free pass for trains and buses and admission to a number of attractions. The trains of Danish State Railways depart from Copenhagen for Funen and Jutland every hour on the hour, and tickets are sold at all railway stations. Discount tickets are available for groups of three or more, for children, for passengers over sixty-five, and for days of the week when traffic is light.

All you need to drive in Denmark is a United States driver's license and a major credit card to rent a car. Roads go everywhere, and you drive on the right side. Border to border from north to south takes only four hours. Gasoline is priced in liters, not gallons. Headlights are turned on day and night, and seatbelts must be worn in front and back seats. Danish law is strict on driving under the influence of alcohol, and foreigners are not excused.

Bicycles are everywhere. You can rent a bicycle, or bring your own. In Copenhagen, major streets have busy bicycle lanes, and in rural areas paved bicycle lanes parallel many roads. You can carry bikes on trains and ferries and on long-distance motor coaches.

Accommodations in Denmark range from a familiar chain to Copenhagen's elegant D'Angleterre, which has been welcoming guests since 1755. You may choose a centuries-old Danish manor house called a *slot,* take a guest room in a farmhouse, book a holiday house at the beach, or relax in a *kro,* an inn similar to the American bed and breakfast.

Children are delighted to see wonders like Legoland Park, the Danish Cycle Museum, amusement parks with thrill rides, circuses, and the seals at the North Sea Museum in Hirtshals.

Venture out of the city to see *Hamlet* at Kronberg Castle and meet ghosts in the long, gleaming Knights' Hall. Find a fairy-tale castle—Frederiksborg, Egeskov, or Rosenholm.

Lounge on the beaches of North Jutland. White sand is everywhere, but the calmer waters are on the east coast. Visit the haunted Forest of Rold, the bird cliffs of Bulbjerg where kittiwakes breed, and Vejlerne, the largest bird sanctuary in northern Europe.

A visit to the museums in Skagen, Denmark's northernmost town, affords a satisfying look into the work of some of Denmark's Impressionist painters: Ann and Michael Anchers' domestic scenes with a Renoir glow; P.S. Krøyer's Victorians, both elegant and convivial in gardens and on beaches, and

Laurits Tuxen's subtle, moody landscapes.

Aalborg, the principal city of North Jutland, boasts a museum of fine art and numerous historical museums, as well as a cathedral built in 1400. There's also a Viking burial ground and a high viewing tower. Night life is exciting in Aalborg, and there's an amusement park named Tivoliland. Called the "Little Paris of the North," Aalborg has something for everyone.

On the Island of Funen, visit the museum of Hans Christian Andersen, visit his hometown of Odense, and see the lovely swans on the quiet river— former ugly ducklings.

Even if you have no relatives in Denmark, the Danes will make you feel like family. Tourism is such an important industry that they want you to enjoy yourself and tell your friends. If you don't have family in Denmark, Friends Overseas will match you with Danes of similar interests for a small fee. Send your name, address, phone number, age, occupation, and when and where you plan to visit to: Friends Overseas (W), 68-01 Dartmouth Street, Forest Hills, New York 11375. Include a stamped, self-addressed envelope or visit: www.friendsoverseas.org for more information.

And when you're in Denmark, don't forget to look up. Some of the most magnificent scenery is the ever-changing spectacle of the Danish sky.

The Enchantment of Legoland

A showcase for the wondrous Lego toys is a park in the small town of Billund, in central Jutland. The park was opened in 1968 by Godfred Kirk Christiansen, whose father, Ole Kirk Christiansen, created the small interlocking plastic bricks in 1955. The park draws a million visitors a year. It is open from May 1 through the third Sunday of September. Indoor exhibits are open all year.

The park is filled with models such as those Christiansen's design team builds for toy shops around the world. One feature in the park is a replica of Gutzon Borglum's Mount Rushmore Memorial. It was created by Danish artist Bjorn Richter, who had visited Mount Rushmore in the 1970s. This project took a year and a half, and involved applying a special glue to each of the 1.5 million tiny white bricks. In 1978, Richter added an art relief, "The Big Bison Hunt," using 2.7 million bricks to create bison of several sizes. Then he created a huge image of Chief Sitting Bull. All these wonders are in a setting of frontier flavor—a general store, the Pony Express, and a saloon—in a Wild West town where children can pan for gold and buy headbands of feathers.

Elsewhere in the park is Miniland, depicting Hamlet's castle, the Austrian Alps, the Statue of Liberty, the United States Capitol in Washington, D.C., the launching pad at Cape Canaveral, Florida, Copenhagen's Nyhavn, and quaint houses surrounded by dwarf plants.

A statue of Hans Christian Andersen made from little gray bricks near the park entrance seems ready to speak. Perhaps only he could explain the magic of making curved facial contours from little angular bricks.

Two Legoland parks have been opened in the United States, one in Carlsbad, California, and the other in Winter Haven, Florida. Legoland California opened March 20, 1999. The park features Dino Island, a miniature roller coaster that travels around giant Lego dinosaurs; Fun Town, a role-playing attraction that allows children to simulate adult or professional roles, such as the Fire Academy, Sky Patrol, and Driving Schools; Castle Hill, a medieval castle-themed area; Miniland U.S.A., which contains scale models of important architecture across America, built over three years with forty million Lego bricks; Pirate Shores, containing six rides and attractions; and a water park. Legoland Florida opened October 15, 2011, and contains more than fifty rides, shows, and attractions based on those at other Legoland parks.

The Mall of America just south of Minneapolis, Minnesota, features its own Lego exhibition that rises through four floors. It has models of dinosaurs, space ships, circus architectural columns and arches, and play areas where children can build toys and skyscrapers with the baby bricks.

Karen Tripp, Houston, Texas, attorney, visited Legoland in Carlsbad, California. Since Karen's visit in 2012, the child-appealing Legoland Hotel opened in the spring of 2013 on Legoland Drive.

—59

Those Irresistible Trolls

"So ugly they're cute" is an oft-heard description of the wild-haired troll dolls created by Thomas Dam of Gjol, Denmark. Trolls are more prominent in Norwegian than in Danish folklore, but the Danes have added their own humorous twist. It is said that a kind old troll lived with his huge family in a cave that was too crowded. They decided to move into another one, and the old troll tried to cast a spell that would make his family bigger and stronger for the task. Something went wrong, however, and they began to shrink. The tiny creatures ran out of the cave and made their smiling way into the world.

At least four United States manufacturers have produced Dam's trolls and other companies bought licensing rights for related items. Lawsuits were brought claiming that some manufacturers copied the Dam troll face, but the bright-eyed trolls smiled on, dressed as cheerleaders, astronauts, football players, and even brides. Dam's "Things from Denmark" became something big.

The Truth About the "Great Dane"

The only Great Danes that Denmark can claim are humans. The American Kennel Club insists that there is "no known reason for connecting Denmark with either the origin or the development of this dog breed." Called "one of the most elegant and distinguished varieties of giant-type dog," the Great Dane is a mastiff with a heavy head for fighting or hunting.

The French called the breed *grand Danois,* meaning "big Danish," but they also called it *dogue allemand* or "German Mastiff." The breed was "made in Germany," and German fanciers bred the finest specimens. The Great Dane has been a distinct type for more than 400 years and was used to tackle wild boars.

Some Germans have tried to abolish the "Great Dane" name, but English-speaking people have stubbornly retained it. Somehow it sounds more distinguished than *Deutsche* Doggie.

The Glorious Fourth in Denmark

The Rebild Festival, the largest Fourth of July observance outside the United States, has been celebrated since 1912 except during World Wars I and II. The setting is the heathered hills of Rebild National Park south of Aalborg, Denmark, several hundred acres of moorland purchased in 1911 by immigrants who called themselves the Danish American Association. One of the prime movers in establishing the park and the celebration was Max Henius, a Danish chemist who came to the United States in 1886.

In 1934, a park was enhanced by construction of a replica of the log cabin in which Abraham Lincoln was born. It was built of timbers from forests throughout the United States. This, too, was a gift to the Danish nation from immigrants in America and their descendants. The park maintains an emigrant archives building and an emigration museum.

The Stars and Stripes and the *Dannebrog* fly from twin flagpoles on the slopes of Rebild, where up to 40,000 people are seated each July 4 to hear singing and speaking in two languages.

Many, including Danish monarchs, have spoken at Rebild on the subject of the long, warm relationship between the two nations.

The Rebild Festival is the occasion for elegant dining, *al fresco* or otherwise, on something like cold salmon and white wine. Danes say they celebrate a foreign holiday with such enthusiasm in order to get some of their relatives back home for a visit, to affirm the values they share with Americans (the right to make one's way in the world unhampered), and to experience what they call "the family of Greater Denmark." There is a July 4 evening party at Aalborg Hall, Aalborg, and the Festival ends with speeches and fireworks in the city's Kilde Park.

Why is this relationship so strong? Maybe it's simply because more than one-eighth of all people in Denmark (some say nearly one-fourth) moved to the United States in the nineteenth and twentieth centuries.

Paper cutting by Hans Christian Andersen

Danish Modern and the Pleasures of Porcelain

One of the greatest influences on American interiors and furnishings has been Danish design. The Danish Modern style began when the cabinet makers of Denmark employed the best designers in Copenhagen to create a distinctively Danish style. When form marries function, the offspring is beauty. Many of these designers had been students of Kaare Klint (1888–1954), an architect who opened new concepts in designing sculptured solid-wood furniture that was functional and beautiful. In 1924, Klint founded the Danish Academy of Art and became its professor of furniture design. Klint strongly influenced a generation of leading designers, including architect Finn Juhl and Hans Wegner. One prototype for industrialized production was Juhl's teakwood chair with open arms and a sparsely upholstered sculptured frame. Another was Wegner's chair inspired by a Chinese child's chair.

Edgar Kaufmann, Jr., of the Museum of Modern Art in New York, returned from Europe in 1948 with photographs of Juhl's chairs. A major exhibit of "The Arts of Denmark" at the Metropolitan Museum in New York in the fall of 1960 helped make Danish Modern all the rage. New designs, such as Arne Jacobsen's "egg" and "swan" chairs of upholstered plastic and Paul Kjaerholm's steel chairs combined with leather or wicker, simplified form and yet made it expressive, humanizing the Bauhaus tradition. As author Villy Sørensen has said, "Getting more of something is good, but getting something good is better."

Skilled craftsmen blend the old with the new, fitting heirlooms into the light, bright sweep of contemporary lines. A glowing piece of Royal Copenhagen porcelain from the last century may be paired with Georg Jensen's sleek contemporary casserole. Jensen, who produced *faience* (earthenware decorated with opaque colored glazes) before opening a jewelry and silverware shop in Copenhagen in 1904, was the chief proponent of distinguished modern forms based on old Scandinavian crafts. There is confusion about the first porcelain made in Denmark. It was once common to refer to all *faience* as Delf's porcelain, even though it was not porcelain at all.

In 1752 and 1757, the ivory carver Christoph Ludwig Lück and his son Karl were granted royal subsidies to make porcelain. Jürgen Gulding and Johann Gottlieb Melhorn received subsidies in 1753 and 1754. Melhorn produced a blue and white ware. Niels Birch found kaolin, a white clay, on the island of Bornholm in 1755, and the Danish porcelain industry was well on its way. A Frenchman named Fournier produced soft paste at Blaataarn between 1760 and 1765. He produced useful wares painted with a French style, but King Frederik V closed that factory a month before his death in 1765.

Fournier's secrets were given to J.G. Richter, a painter from Strasborg, and Frantz Heinrich Müller. In 1772, they received 1,000 rigsdalers to start a factory. The dowager queen Juliane Marie became their patroness, and in 1775, they received a five-year monopoly. Their mark was three wave-shaped lines representing the Sound and the Great and the Little Belts of Denmark.

The factory, producing bluish-gray ware, became *Den Kongelige Danske Porcelains Fabrik,* or Royal Copenhagen, in 1779.

The famous Flora Danica service was to be a gift to Catherine the Great of Russia, but she died before it was completed. Each piece was decorated with a botanical painting by Johan Christoph Bayer, whose eyesight was ruined on the set. The work began in 1789. In 1802, although it was uncompleted, work was stopped at 2,600 pieces.

About 1,800 pieces of this precious porcelain were used at a birthday reception for King Christian VII in 1803. The surviving 1,530 pieces are on display at Rosenborg Castle in Copenhagen. A second, much smaller Flora Danica set of 765 pieces was created as a wedding gift for Princess Alexandria of Denmark and Edward, Prince of Wales.

Royal Copenhagen became famous for its pure white biscuit-fired figurines, reduced scale copies of works by neoclassical sculptor Bertel Thorvaldsen. The company's strongest rival came from within. In 1853, Frederik Wilhelm Grøndahl, who had been a modeler in the Royal Copenhagen firm, went into business with two stationers and book sellers, Jacob and Meyer Bing. By the turn of the century, Bing and Grøndahl were showing the work of two famous sculptors—Kai Nielsen and Jean Gauguin, one of four children born to the French painter and his Danish wife, the former Mette Sophie Gad, during their twelve years of marriage (1873–1885). In 1895, Bing and Grøndahl became the first to issue a commemorative Christmas plate. The price was fifty cents. A century later, that plate could be sold for $4,000. Royal Copenhagen did not produce its first Christmas plate—priced at $1.00—until 1908. Rounding out a century of blue-gray *Jul* greetings—bells, Christmas trees, angels, step-gable churches, and all the images of Christmas—both companies charged $54.90 for the 1985 edition. In 1987, the two companies merged with a third, Holmegaard, under the name

Royal Copenhagen. Their 2012 Christmas plate, depicting a sailboat, is priced at $89.00.

Danish Christmas plates are a good investment, but that's not why so many Danish-American homes are galleried with the soft blue beauties. They tie our hearts to the homeland.

The development of Danish art glass is comparatively recent, dating from the 1970s. Finn Lynggaard started the Danish movement to create studio glass. His own work combines strong, rich colors with clear glass.

2013 marks the 100th anniversary of the famous Little Mermaid statue in the Copenhagen Harbour in Denmark. The Little Mermaid *is a fairy tale by the Danish author Hans Christian Andersen.*

Image courtesy The Danish Windmill
Copenhagen Harbour Plate

Villy Sørensen

Is it harmless to trick the reader into thinking? Or can a simple story be just that—simple? If titling a group of short stories *Harmless Tales* fails to lend a hint, possibly it is because Villy Sørensen's writings are different. Then again, perhaps it is because his stories did not become available in English until long after they had been translated into most European languages.

Born in Copenhagen in 1929, Villy Sørensen has been named *Doctor honoris causa* of the University of Copenhagen. Among many other honors, in 1986 he became the first to be awarded the Swedish Academy Prize for Scandinavian authors, often called "the Little Nobel."

Thus Sørensen is a serious writer, although a first reader might be forgiven for wondering upon reading of tenants each of whom picks up a wall and walks away as the astonished landlord stands watching, and they all head for the new high-rise where no one wants to live. Different? Yes. Humorous? Yes, but remember—"harmless." Challenging? Read closely.

A Fairy Tale Life

Through his famous fairy tales, Hans Christian Andersen became the darling of the princely courts of Europe and the commoners everywhere. The son of an Odense shoemaker, he was born in 1805 in "a poor little room" two months after his parents' wedding. He often said his own life was a fairy tale, but some of the magical rewards of such a life eluded him. For one thing, he wanted to write successful plays, and the satisfaction was denied him. For another, he never won the hand of the princess.

Physically, Andersen was an ugly duckling who never became a swan. His extremely prominent nose, heavy-lidded eyes, and fleshy lips give him a singular appearance that stirred no admiration in women. Even so, hoping for a more appealing likeness, he had himself painted and photographed repeatedly.

He came from Funen, where the dialect is "the language spoken by the angels on Sunday." His mother was of illegitimate birth and close to illiterate, but loving. She washed other people's clothes in the river to support herself and her son. His father fought for Napoleon and died when Hans was eleven. The most normal family member was his paternal grandmother, and she had delusions of grandeur and gentility that left their mark on the boy. Her husband was feeble-minded, making a spectacle of himself in the streets. Young Hans worried about inheriting this affliction.

When the Royal Theatre visited Odense in 1818 for a guest performance, Andersen, at age thirteen, was smitten by the magic of the stage and vowed to go to Copenhagen. He did just that when he was fourteen, taking acting and singing lessons. Neither art was his long suit, and his last hope was writing drama. He received a withering rejection of his first effort, the theater owner saying he "desired to receive no more pieces which, like this one, betray a lack of elementary education." He tried and was rejected again, but he had an uncanny ability to make useful contacts. He found a patron at the theatre who got him a grant to attend grammar school.

Andersen's first love was Riborg Voigt, a brown-eyed girl from the south of Funen who refused his proposal of marriage. He later proposed to Louise Collin, the daughter of his financial counselor, and to Jenny Lind, the Swedish Nightingale. Both refused him, but Jenny Lind remained his warm and helpful friend. When Andersen died, a letter to him was found in a leather pouch around his neck. It was the farewell letter of his first love, Riborg Voigt. By his order, it was burned unread.

Andersen was one of the most traveled men of his time. Having a deep fear of dying by fire, he always traveled with a stout rope to be used in escaping a burning hotel room. He also was afraid of dogs and of missing his train. He particularly loved Italy, writing, "What Germany and the North are for the heart, and France for the intelligence, Italy is for the imagination." Italy inspired his novel, *The Improvisatore,* which was a great success. Yet his fairy tales outshone and outlasted his other writings. He could capture a world of truth in a tiny tale. His first book of fairy tales was an unpretentious little volume, *Fairy Tales Told For Children,* and with it he had arrived at the form that would win for him the hearts of the world. First, he retold stories he had heard as a child. Then he invented his own, including *The Little Mermaid, The Storks,* and *The Daisy.* Between 1835 and 1872, he published more than 150 fairy tales. A Danish translator protested in the 1990s that an English-language publisher was "sanitizing" the words of *The Nightingale* to protect the tender minds of young American readers! Andersen, who made the fantastic real and the real fantastic, would not have understood that. All life was miraculous to him. He wrote, "The fairy tale is the most extensive realm of poetry, ranging from the blood-smoking graves of the past to the pious picture book of childish legend, absorbing folk literature and art literature."

Critics have found parallels from Andersen's life in his fairy tales, calling *The Ugly Duckling* and *The Fir Tree* autobiographical, seeing his mother's death in *She Was Good for Nothing,* finding his childhood home in *Holger Danske,* and linking his new boots for confirmation to *The Red Shoes.* His romances with Riborg Voigt, Louise Collin, and Jenny Lind can be seen in *Sweethearts, The Little Mermaid,* and *Under The Willow Tree.*

Andersen wrote, "I seize on an idea for older people and then tell it to the younger ones, while remembering that Father and Mother are listening and must have something to think about." He wrote for whole families, and there was a smile in his art, but there were shadows, too.

When Hans Christian Andersen died in 1875, he left that rich legacy to the whole world. The home where Andersen was born is open for visitors, and the museum in Odense (pronounced O-den-see with the accent on the "O") features his life in books in many languages, and displays his paper cuttings.

The Story of the Little Mermaid

The bronze figure of Hans Christian Andersen's Little Mermaid in Copenhagen's harbor is tiny and lovely. Replicas of the Eriksen sculpture in Solvang, California, and Kimballton, Iowa, are appreciated because the predominately Danish populations know the Little Mermaid's story.

She lives with her father, the Merman King; five older sisters; and her grandmother in an undersea palace, awaiting her 15th birthday, when she will rise from the sea and view the moonlit world.

When the longed-for time arrives, she swims up to a ship, looks through the porthole, and loses her heart to a handsome prince celebrating his birthday. A terrible storm strikes the ship, but the Little Mermaid saves the prince, and they float ashore near a temple. Maidens from the temple discover the prince and lead him away.

The Little Mermaid grieved, thinking she could have kept him at her side if she were human and with an immortal soul, but mermaids don't have souls. They live for 300 years, then become foam on the water. Her grandmother has told her that she can gain a soul if a human loves her more than he loves his parents and marries her, but humans want wives with legs, not fish tails. The Little Mermaid bargains with a sea-witch, trading her lovely voice for legs that will encourage the prince to propose. If he marries another, she will die the next day.

They meet again, but he marries one of the temple maidens, thinking it was she who saved his life. Now the Little Mermaid must kill the prince to save her own life, but when her five sisters offer a knife, she throws it back into the sea and meets her foamy fate bravely. She takes the shape of ethereal beings floating above her.

In about 300 years, these airy creatures may float into Paradise, but first, they float into homes. For each good child they find, a year is removed from their time of trial. A bad child makes them cry, each tear adding a day to their wanderings.

The Chimney Sweep and the Shepherdess

The fairy tale figures formerly atop the Danish Inn Restaurant in Solvang, California, are Hans Christian Andersen's china lovers, the Shepherdess and the Chimney Sweep.

Their romance begins on a parlor table chaperoned by an old Chinaman who can nod his head and claims to be the Shepherdess's grandfather. She also has an unwanted suitor, a goatish creature called "Top-and-bottom-general-commander-in-chief-sergeant-billy-goats" by the children of the house, and when he asks for her hand, the Chinaman nods.

The Sweep and the Shepherdess run away together, using his small ladder to climb from the table and ascend through the stove and chimney to the roof. The wide world below is so frightening to the Shepherdess that her tears wash the gold from her sash.

They crawl back down the chimney and discover the old Chinaman in three pieces. He has fallen in trying to follow them. When he is riveted and glued together, he can no longer nod approving the repeated proposals of the goatish suitor. The lovers live happily—not ever after, but until they are broken to bits—a rueful piece of realism in a fairy tale.

These paper cuts are by Hans Christian Andersen. They are meant to be pleasing to look at and also thought provoking. He made them to be entertaining to his friends and their children.

Out of Africa: The Baroness

On a trip to Denmark many years ago, I bought a poster that was Cecil Beaton's portrait of Karen Blixen in a black cloche. The Danish red ground was lettered with her name and that of her Danish publisher, Gyldendal. She had many other names. Her most famous was Isak Dinesen. The aristocratic face watched over me and my typewriter until the poster was faded and torn. I took it down in 1985, when Americans were watching Meryl Streep play the famous Danish author in the film, *Out of Africa,* made from Dinesen's 1937 book of the same title. (Royalties from that film paid the bills as Dinesen's former home at Rungsted, Denmark, was made into a museum.) Although I had memorized her face, I did not know her work as well. I reveled in the 1987 prize-winning film, *Babette's Feast,* not knowing it was made from a story by Isak Dinesen. Born April 17, 1885, the author-to-be was christened Karen Christentze. From her earliest years she was strong-willed. She believed there was a divine intention to life and was forever searching for a more intense experience. This sense of self enabled her to prevail in many kinds of adversity, including the suicide of her father, Wilhelm Dinesen, when she was ten.

Tanne, as her family called her, went to a private drawing school. While there, she fasted herself gaunt, saying that excess weight cramped her style. In 1903, she was accepted for study at the Royal Academy of Fine Arts in Copenhagen. She began writing Gothic tales, emphasizing the supernatural in a medieval setting. Her story, *The Hermits,* was published in 1907 under the pseudonym Osceola, the name of her father's German shepherd. Falling in love with her cousin, Hans Blixen, who was the prototype for Hemingway's great white hunter (Robert Wilson, in *The Short Happy Life of Francis Macomber)*, she found that her feelings were not reciprocated, and in 1912 married his twin, Baron Bror, becoming the Baroness Blixen-Finecke. The couple went to Africa, where her family's money bought them a "coffee plantation." A favorite wedding present, a Scottish Deerhound named Dusk, went with them. Unfortunately, they did not know the conditions were wrong for coffee.

Known in Africa as Tania, she made the plantation house into a villa but kept to herself. During World War I, the English thereabouts believed her to be a German spy, but she was later to host the Prince of Wales, who became King of England and then the Duke of Windsor. "Tania" was appreciated by the Africans. She loved to go on safari and "shoot her own fur coats," but soon hunted only for food for the Africans, or to kill lions, often at the request of the Africans. She sent a rare black-maned lion skin to King Christian X. Several of her friends laughed at her, but the king accepted the gift with thanks. In 1914, she was very ill with what she thought was malaria. Instead, it was syphilis contracted from her husband, and she went home to Denmark to be treated with mercury. Yearning for Africa, she returned there as soon as her health improved. In 1918, she met Denys Finch-Hatton, an unconventional English charmer seeking African adventure. He became the real love of her life. When he came to dinner, they dressed formally. She dramatized her eyes with kohl and made them shine with belladonna.

Then the losses began. In 1922, Bror Blixen asked for a divorce. They were forced to sell the farm, Finch-Hatton died in a plane crash, and she went back to Denmark, leaving the crates from Africa unopened for thirteen years. She resumed writing, taking the name Isak, which means "he who laughs." She preferred to deal with the past, finding a finished world complete in all its elements. Her book *Seven Gothic Tales* was the February Book-of-the-Month selection in 1934, published by Harrison Smith and Robert Haas, a firm that later merged with Random House. No one knew who Isak Dinesen was, but they finally tracked her down. She wrote in English and did her own Danish translation because she was dissatisfied with the work of others. Her book about Africa was taking shape, not as a documentary, but as an overview with real-life events rearranged. *Out of Africa* was her second Book-of-the-Month selection—in the late 1930s. During World War II, she wrote *Winter's Tales,* the "most Danish" of her books. Her story, *Babette's Feast,* was the result of a bet with an English friend. Challenged by his wager that she couldn't write anything acceptable to the *Saturday Evening Post,* she took his advice, "Write about food. Americans are obsessed with it." The story was an exquisite comedy rejected by the *Post* but published by the *Ladies Home Journal.*

Much of the author's stomach was removed early in 1953 and she "planned to die" in 1955, but it didn't work that way. In 1958, she enjoyed being a literary celebrity in the United States, where, among other experiences, she met Marilyn Monroe at the home of author Carson McCullers and consumed oysters and champagne. For the last months of her life in the summer of 1962, she subsisted on juice, *gelée royale,* oysters, and dry biscuits, dying of malnutrition September 7, 1962. She left behind a reverberation of her strong belief, "True art is always part magic." Decades later, the magic remains. Although the poster is gone from my wall, I still feel the burning gaze of those hooded eyes set deep in the face of Tanne, Osceola, Scheherazade, Tania, Karen, Isak—the Baroness.

Out of Isaac Dinesen

by Linda Donelson

In 1985 the movie *Out of Africa* introduced more than fifty million people around the world to Karen Blixen's fascinating life. I was then a young mother intensely interested in learning more about the woman who ran a coffee farm in Kenya at the turn of the century. My husband and I, and our four children, had also lived on a farm in Africa at the foot of the Ngong Hills.

The film marvelously evoked the atmosphere of life in colonial Kenya. Meryl's Streep's portrayal of Karen Blixen seemed very real—even to the color of her hair. Other characters in the film, including Klaus Maria Brandauer as the endearing rogue, Bror Blixen, and Michael Kitchen as the amusing friend Berkeley Cole, appeared to be very close to life. But, as a physician, I recognized that certain elements of the story were pure Hollywood fiction. The true story of the Danish author's life in Kenya is only vaguely sketched in her book, *Out of Africa*. She mentions her husband only once, and she describes the hunter, Denys Finch Hatton, as no more than a friend. She doesn't talk about the syphilis she acquired from her husband in their first year of marriage, nor does she reveal her two miscarried pregnancies with Finch Hatton.

None of the four books used to make the movie—Isak Dinesen's *Letters from Africa, Out of Africa,* and two biographies—give a clear account of the years Karen Blixen spent in Africa, from 1914 to 1931. I wanted to know more. I went on to write the book, *Out of Isak Dinesen* in Africa, that would remain the number one best-selling Scandinavian / or related title for five years at Amazon.com.

Linda Donelson died in 2013. Her hardback biography is available from Penfield Books. Paperback copies are available from Amazon.

Shakespeare Borrowed a Dane

The Bard of Avon, William Shakespeare, created his famous Hamlet, Prince of Denmark, by some astute borrowing. The first mention of the legendary Danish Prince Amleth was made by the twelfth-century Danish historian, Saxo Grammaticus, in his *Historica Danica,* written in Latin. The English playwright Thomas Kyd wrote a version of *Hamlet* that has not survived, and the tale was found in Belleforest's *Histoires Tragiques.*

Shakespeare's *Hamlet* dates from 1602. The play is filled with death, destruction, and revenge, and the Amleth of the original legend certainly was acquainted with these. He was a minor noble who chopped one of his enemies to pieces beneath the straw on the floor and fed the remains to the pigs. On another occasion, he invited his foes to a feast, locked them in the house were they were carousing, and set the place afire.

Shakespeare's Hamlet, a noble fellow, has become real at Elsinore while Amleth has faded from memory. "The play's the real thing," and *Hamlet* can be seen at Kronborg Castle.

Pelle Wins in Real Life

Were it not for the 1988 award-winning Swedish film, *"Pelle the Conqueror,"* few Americans today would be aware of the Danish novelist Martin Andersen Nexø. Based on the novel of the same title, the film was directed by Bille August and starred Max Von Sydow and Pelle Hvenegaard. It won an Oscar, the Golden Globe, and the Golden Palm of the Cannes International Film Festival as the best foreign film of 1988.

The story of Pelle begins in 1877 on the Danish island of Bornholm. Pelle is an eight-year-old motherless boy whose father is elderly and whose environment is harsh, rough, and cruel. Out of these unlikely surroundings, Pelle emerges with the spirit and will to rise above adversity, propelled by his innate joy of being alive. Born in Copenhagen in 1869, Andersen Nexø himself grew up in poverty and came up smiling. He worked as a cobbler's apprentice and a hod carrier before attending the Askov folk high school. A keen observer of life, he was a champion of the proletariat, and has been compared to the Russian writer, Maxim Gorky.

Symphonies of Success

Carl Nielsen (1865–1931) was neither the first nor the last to wonder whether his music would be recognized and lasting. But today, if you turn on your favorite public radio station, you might hear a symphony or concerto by Denmark's foremost composer.

Nielsen wrote six symphonies, two operas—"Saul and David" and "Maskerade"—concertos for clarinet, flute, and violin, and many others, including some fifty hymns written during the spring of 1914 in a successful bid to improve the quality of religious communal singing.

He and his friend, Thomas Laub, collaborated to reform Danish secular song, also with great success, simplifying the style to be generally accessible. Their publication of seventy songs marked a turning point in Danish popular and folk music. Romance and lieder went into decline.

In 1891, Nielsen went to Paris, where he completed the First Symphony. In that same year, he met and married the sculptress Anne Marie Brodersen. The couple had three children.

Nielsen played violin, was music director at the Royal Theatre from 1908 to 1914, was conductor of the Copenhagen Musical Society from 1915 to 1927, and was director of the Royal Conservatory.

Among his woes as he composed his Sixth Symphony was a deep perplexity about the direction of post-World War I music. He included a humoresque that was a savage take-off on what was "new" in music, and a slow movement of despairing lament. One of his last compositions was "Piano Music for Young and Old," a set of twenty-four pieces in all keys, published in 1930.

Nielsen was buried in Vestre Kirkegard, Copenhagen. His wife created a memorial, "The Singing Cherub," erected at his birthplace, Nørre-Lyndelse, in Sortelung, a village near Odense on the Island of Fyn. A museum honors him in Odense. She also created a famous monument in Copenhagen of Pan with his flute, sitting on a wild horse that symbolizes poetry. Pan's face is that of Carl Nielsen.

Christen Købke

In his short lifetime, Christen Købke (1810–1848) experienced anxiety over his progress as an artist, and indeed, his work was virtually unknown outside Denmark for more than a century after his death. Many of his small portraits and landscapes had been given to his friends and relatives. Suddenly, the "discovery" Christen Købke began, probably with the writings of scholars, and his works—however small—were seen in major museums, including the Getty in California and the Metropolitan in New York.

The son of a baker, Købke suffered an illness in his early teens which may have influenced him in later years. He painted in his own distinctive style in his twenties, was less productive in his thirties, and died of pneumonia at age thirty-seven. He had lived nearly all his life with his parents, even after his marriage.

The art critic John Russell wrote in the *New York Times* that Købke's paintings "are what Van Gogh called 'truer than true,' and although they are mostly very small—on average ten by eight inches or so—each bears within itself a whole world, completely realized."

Købke was a contemporary of Hans Christian Andersen, Søren Kierkegaard, and a number of talented poets and painters during the golden era of European cultural history that followed the disruptive years of Napoleon's wars.

An exhibition celebrating "The Golden Age of Danish Painting" was organized by the Los Angeles County Museum of Art and the Metropolitan Museum of Art in New York and was on view in Los Angeles in late 1993 and in New York February 13 through April 24, 1994. It featured 105 works created by artists including Købke, Jens Juel, Christoffer Wilhelm Eckersberg, Christian Rørbye, Constantin Hansen, and Johan Thomas Lundbye. The exhibition gave emphasis to Copenhagen as one of the major artistic centers of Europe in the 1780–1850 period during which these works were painted.

The Romance of Danish Ballet

The Royal Danish Ballet is one of the world's most venerable dance companies. The oldest known choreography of *Romeo and Juliet* was done for the Royal Danish Ballet—in 1811 by Vincenzo Galeotti.

The Bournonvilles, Antoine and his son, August, had the greatest influence on the company. In 1829, August began to put his stamp on the Royal Danish Ballet. The Bournonville tradition, a scintillating blend of choreography and sunny social commentary, has been preserved in its original form because the Bournonville repertoire remained in relative isolation from Denmark until the mid-twentieth century.

Among August Bournonville's romantic ballets is "Napoli," the love story of Teresina and Gennaro, a young fisherman. The lovers are separated, and Teresina is carried into the Blue Grotto, where she is transformed into a naiad. Gennaro seeks and finds her, and she resumes her human form. The people of Naples believe evil witches have arranged Teresina's return until the priest assures them the Blessed Virgin was responsible for the lovers' reunion and the ballet ends with an exhilarating tarantella.

Bournonville was so taken by the romance of the Mediterranean that in 1858 he choreographed "The Flower Festival at Genzano." The full ballet is still performed in Denmark, and its *pas de deux* became part of the repertoire of many ballet companies.

The New York City Ballet grew out of the School for American Ballet, and that's where a branch of the New York-based Danish American Society, which promotes cultural ties between the United States and Denmark, looks for young dancers to send to the homeland for study.

The Danish American National Cultural Exchange (D.A.N.C.E.) awards grants for studying dance in Copenhagen. It has been sending students to Denmark and bringing Danish students to the United States since 1983.

Holidays in Denmark

By Ingrid Marie Christiansen

More than one tourist has arrived at a place eager to go shopping or to visit a museum only to discover that it is a holiday and almost everything is closed. In Denmark, July is the month of the industrial and school vacations. The light nights, *de lyse naetter,* are too precious to spend indoors. Danes take off. Reservations are recommended for trains, ferries, hotels, inns, and camping grounds. A more positive reason to know about the holidays is that you may want to plan your trip to be there when the holiday occurs. With the exception of New Year's Day, the legal holidays are also Christian holy days. No specific date can be given for movable feast days. The following holidays are listed on the calendar of *Faellesforeningen for Danmarks Brugsforeninger (FDB):*

January 1	New Year's Day *(Nytårsdag).* The chimes in the tower of Copenhagen's City Hall strike twelve at midnight and play a tune from the Middle Ages. Danish radio and television carry a fifty-minute church service during which the choir sings *Vaer Velkommen, Herrens Aar* (text by N.F.S. Grundtvig and music by A. P. Berggreen). Then the reigning monarch gives a short New Year's address. Later in the day, people enjoy visiting and eating.
January 6	Holy Three Kings Day *(HelligtreKongersdag),* last of the winter holidays, is celebrated with a party.

February 2   Candlemas *(Kyndelmisse)*. A church festival in commemoration of the presentation of Christ in the temple and the purification of the Virgin Mary. Candles are blessed and carried in celebration. In 1770 Struense* declared this an unnecessary holy day—still on the calendar, but no longer celebrated.

February   *Fastelavnssøndag*, the Sunday before Fasting. Lent is observed forty weekdays from Ash Wednesday until Easter.

February   Shrove Tuesday *(Fastelavn)* is celebrated before Ash Wednesday. This holiday has been the subject of much research. In Denmark, it is celebrated on Monday or during the weekend before Lent. One custom formerly associated with *Fastelavn* may owe its origin to an idea that by exterminating cats, evil would be driven away. In recent times, *Fastelavn* is celebrated by dressing up in costumes and masks. Children visit friends and neighbors and chant a "trick or treat" song. If they cannot be identified, they receive a *Fastelavn* bun or treat. *Fastelavn* resembles the American Halloween more than the riotus Mardi Gras, a pre-Lenten festival climaxing on Shrove Tuesday.

Ash Wednesday *Askeonsdag*. Ashes used in church services are the residue of burned palms from the previous Palm Sunday. Ash is a symbol of repentence.

February 10   *Afstemningsdag*. The 1920 election that restored Sønderjylland to Danish rule is celebrated in South Jutland with speeches, singing, and refreshments.

March   The Spring equinox *(Jaevndøgn)*, when the sun crosses the equator and the day and the night are equal in length, occurs the third week of March.

March 28   Queen Ingrid's birthday—mother of the reigning queen.

* Johann Friedrich Struense (1737–1772), physician to the mentally troubled Christian VII. Struense was arrested and killed for becoming the queen's lover.

March	Palm Sunday *(Palmsøndag)*, or Maundy Thursday *(Skaetorsdag)*
April	Good Friday *(Langfredag)*. Easter Sunday *(Paaskesøndag)*. The first Sunday after the first full moon after the spring equinox. Easter Monday *(2 Paaskedag)*.
April 9	Occupation day *(Besættelsesdag)* marks the date of the occupation of Denmark by Nazi Germany in World War II. Flags are at half-staff.
April 16	The Queen's birthday. There are special ceremonies in Amalienborg Square, where the Danish Royal Guards perform. Crowds cheer and sing the Danish birthday songs, as well as the American "Happy Birthday" song. The birth of Queen Margrethe II in 1940, a week after the Nazi occupation of Denmark, was considered a token of hope by the Danish people. The Royal family, especially her grandfather King Christian X, served as a symbol to all Danes that they should remain proud of their identity and not be defeated in spirit by the hardships imposed under foreign rule.
April 18	*Dybbølsdag* commemorates the battle of Dybbol (1864) where the small defending Danish army was vanquished by the larger German force. Memorial services are held at the site.
May 1	Workers International Day *(Arbejdernesdag)*. In the morning before work, union leaders address the members. Many factory workers get a free half-day. In the afternoon, the Social Democratic party holds meetings, and everyone has a jolly good time. Before the Labor movement took over this holiday, it was celebrated with Maypole festivities instead of political rallies.
May 4	Commemorates the night before the Danish liberation. Lighted candles show in windows everywhere.

May 5	Liberation day *(Danmarks Befrielsesdag)*. On May 5, 1945, Denmark was liberated from German rule. Memorial services *(Højtideligheder)* are held. Lighted candles are placed in windows as a symbol of hope.
The Fourth Friday after Easter	Prayer day *(Store Bededag)*. The fourth Friday after Easter. In earlier times, at least seven prayer days were on the calendar. King Christian VI thought that was too many, and in 1684 they were combined into one *"bod-og bededag"* (confess and pray day).
Forty days after Easter	Ascension Day *(Kristi Himmselfartsdag)* comes forty days after Easter, always on a Thursday.
Seventh Sunday after Easter	Pentecost *(Pinsen),* a Christian feast on the seventh Sunday after Easter, commemorates the descent of the Holy Spirit on the Apostles.
Seventh Sunday plus one day	Second Pentecost day *(2 Pinsedag),* Monday, is an official holiday. Seventh Sunday after Easter plus one day
May 26	Crown Prince Frederik's birthday (born 1968) is usually celebrated at Fredensborg Castle, the royal summer residence. In 1993, it was celebrated by the Danish Society of Massachusetts at Harvard University, where a fund was established in his name to help qualified Danish students spend a year studying at the Kennedy School of Government, as Prince Frederik did.
June 5	Constitution Day *(Grundlovsdag)*. Celebrates the Danish Constitution and the first free election in 1849 with political rallies and an address by the Queen on radio and TV. There are parades, music, flags, and picnics—a half-day holiday.
June 7	Prince Joachim's birthday. Younger brother of Prince Frederik.
June 11	Prince Henrik's birthday. He married the Queen in 1967.

| June 15 | Denmark's flag day *(Valdemarsdag)*. |
| | Reunification Day *(Genforeningsdag)*. On this date, after the 1920 election, King Christian X rode over the border into northern Schlesvig, which had been German-controlled since 1864. |

| June 15 | Summer solstice *(Solhverv)*. The longest day of the year. The solstice occurs when the sun is at its northernmost distance from the equator in its apparent seasonal path, about June 22. |

| June 24 | Saint John the Baptist's Day *(Sankt Hans Dag)*. In Denmark, the Midsummer is celebrated on Saint Hans Evening or the weekend closest to the Summer solstice. People gather for a picnic. After dark, a bonfire with an effigy of a witch on top is set ablaze. Concealed in the witch's clothes is a rocket-like firecracker which fires her off to *Bloksbjerg,* a mountain in the Black Forest. |

| July 4 | American Independence Day has been celebrated since 1912 in Rebild Park. The Rebild Society is an active Danish-American organization with chapters around the U.S.A. |

| July 22 | Dog days *(Hundedagene)* begin. They end August 23. A period when the sea is likely to be calm. Named for the Dog Star, Sirius, it is important in sailing. |

| September 22 | The fall equinox *(Jaevndøgn)* occurs when the day and night are equal in length. It marks the beginning of fall and the harvest celebrations *(høstgilde)*. |

| October 24 | United Nations Day *(FN dag)* is observed by flying the U.N. flag. At the City Hall in Copenhagen, the flags of the U.N. nations are flown. Danish soldiers are part of the U.N. peacekeeping forces. |

| November | All Souls Day *(Alle helgensdag)*. The first Sunday in November commemorates the Reformation and the dead. |

In many churches, the name of parishioners who died within the past year are read aloud.

November 11   Bishop Morten's Day *(Bishop Mortensdag)*. Bishop Martin of Tours (circa A.D. 320–400) became the first European saint in 650. Martin Luther, born November 11, 1483, was named for Saint Martin. According to H.H. Skaaning (1616),when the people of Tours elected Saint Martin to become their bishop, he hid in a goose pen. Because the noisy geese revealed his hiding place, the Bishop decreed that every year on November 11, all households should slaughter their fattest goose as a punishment to geese.

December   Advent *(Advent)*. Advent candles are lighted in the churches the last four Sundays before Christmas. The use of Advent wreaths became common in the 1930s. The custom of giving children a little gift each day of the Advent season became popular in the 1950s. Tourist shops sell Advent calendars, candles, wall hangings, and decorations.

December 13   Saint Lucia's Day *(Sankt Lucia dag)*. Although this popular Swedish festival is not listed on the Danish calendar, it has been celebrated since the 1930s by women's groups and Girl Scouts who arrange Lucia festivals *(Lucia Uptog)* in nursing homes. Words of the songs have been translated into Danish.

December   The winter solstice *(Solhverv)*, the shortest day of the year, occurs about December 21.

December 24   Christmas Eve *(Juleaften)*. So many people go to church that there are often two and three services. After dinner, family members join hands and walk around the lighted Christmas tree singing familiar Christmas songs before presents are opened.

December 25   Christmas Day *(Juledag)*. The birthday of Jesus is celebrated with church services and family visits.

December 26   Second Christmas Day *(2 Juledag).*

December 31   New Year's Eve *(Nytaarsaften).* The Queen, the reigning monarch, gives a talk at 6 p.m.

The legal holidays are New Year's Day, Maundy Thursday, Good Friday, Easter Sunday and Monday, General Prayer Day, Ascension Day, Pentecost Sunday and Monday, Constitution Day (one-half day June 5), Christmas Day, and Second Christmas Day.

God Jul Merry Christmas

If you're Danish, you'll be thinking about Christmas in January—not the Christmas just past, but the one to come. Hans Christian Andersen described a Danish Christmas as "magnificent, quite unforgettably magnificent," and that takes planning. Although you have been buying gifts and tucking them away all through the calendar, October brings real mobilization. That's when letters and greetings are written to be sent abroad.

The annual Christmas seal design is eagerly awaited. One of the loveliest, created by Queen Margrethe, portrayed musical angels and was called "Heaven Prepares for Christmas." The Christmas seal tradition originated in Denmark and Sweden. The advent wreath, formerly ribboned with purple, was changed to the Danish national colors—red and white—because of the passionate patriotism inspired by World War II. Its first candle is lit the fourth Sunday before Christmas.

A tall calendar candle is lit December 1, burning the first of 24 sections marking the days until Christmas. Cardboard houses with 24 windows to be opened or tapestries with tiny gifts hanging from 24 hooks are other ways Danes mark time in the Yuletide season. Early in December, families start to make decorations at "cut and paste" parties. They create cones, baskets, angels, birds, and hearts for the Christmas tree.

Even the birds have their edible decorations—ears of corn hang in a tree or from a balcony. Traditionally, the Christmas tree was chosen and secured on a hike into the woods early in December. It would not be put up and decorated until Christmas Eve. While they wait for that glorious night, the Danes cook and bake. The heavy-duty cooking must wait for "Little Christmas," celebrated before Christmas Day, when the goose will be roasting, the rice pudding keeping its lucky almond secret (the finder wins a prize plus good luck in the coming year), and the red cabbage steaming.

When the glorious tree is revealed, the family joins hands around it to sing carols before opening the beautifully wrapped gifts. No amount of prior poking and shaking will reveal the contents of those packages, because sizes and shapes have been artfully disguised. When all the giving and receiving comes to an end, there's a contentment with music, sweets, fruit, and nuts.

Historically, before bedtime, a dish of porridge was carried to the attic for the *nisse,* the elfish creature who controls domestic fortunes and is not above accepting bribes.

A huge lunch on Christmas Day goes on for hours, beer and schnapps flowing freely, and then the hardiest wrap up for a long walk in the snow— if there is any. The marathon eating goes on into December 26, Boxing Day, and the Danes will cling to Christmas through Twelfth Night, when they light three candles as a substitute for the Christmas tree. The birds are now enjoying the new decorations of suet and nuts outside.

An old Danish song asserts that "the Christmas season lasts until Easter," and perhaps it does. Children often say, "I wish Christmas would last forever," and the Danes almost make that wish come true.

The Lesser Christmas Miracle

It's easy for an Iowa child to believe what my Danish grandmother told me— that the farm animals celebrate the birth of Christ with human utterance at midnight on Christmas Eve. I first believed it on a farm near Fiscus, and it flowed like a sweet undercurrent beneath the many holiday preparations.

A piece had to be learned for the Christmas program at Merrill's Grove Baptist Church, and I was admonished not to twist the hem of my skirt to immodest heights while delivering it. I performed without a lapse of memory and left my hemline alone, and when the program was over, we all got brown paper bags filled with hard candy. The bumpy raspberries with soft centers were my favorites, but I also admired the small rounds with a flower that remained visible until the candy was sucked to a sliver.

I had plans to visit the barn at midnight to hear what the cattle had to say to each other, but I kept them to myself, sensing that I would be thwarted should anyone find out. The paradoxically soft and stark light of the kerosene lamps shone on the clock face I could not yet read, and I asked again and again, "Is it midnight yet?" I had never experienced a midnight, and that prospect plus talking animals was almost too much excitement to bear.

My parents spoke of Santa Claus, which presented a problem. If I went to the barn at midnight to listen to the animals, Santa Claus would have to wait to bring my presents, and he might not be able to work me into his route. What to do?

Exhaustion solved my dilemma. I awoke in my own bed in the cold light of Christmas morning and hurried to the dining room to see what Santa had brought with no more than a fleeting regret about missing the animal conversation. There would be other years, other midnights. Now there was the joy of a small table painted bright orange and a sack of peanuts in the shell. The gifts seemed wonderful to me, and I had no notion of the thought and struggle that went into them in that Depression year. For years I did not know that my father made the table from an apple box, a broomstick, and the core of a linoleum roll, or that finding a few cents to buy peanuts involved looking through pockets and old purses for forgotten coins.

Later in the morning I went to the barn, hoping that the cattle still might have the power to speak, but they didn't. I had missed the moment, and now they only chewed and exhaled their grain-sweet breath in my face.

"I'll come next year," I said, but I never did. That was my last Christmas on the farm, and my father's last Christmas on earth. We moved to town.

In Harlan, Christmas meant colored lights strung from the Shelby County Courthouse like a brilliant spider web, blue electric candles in Aunt Mary's window, and in Grandma's house, where we were living, a Christmas tree with wax candles—so lovely and so dangerous. We walked the streets of the town and admired the electric lights in other people's windows. There were other Christmases in other houses, and for our family, hard times persisted, but they didn't seem so hard at the time. One year when we couldn't afford a Christmas tree, we cut a bough from the huge pine on the family cemetery plot and thrust it into a crock of sand. Then we punctured our fingers stringing popcorn and cranberries and made chains of paper loops to decorate the "tree." The bough smelled as a Christmas tree should, but it also wept resin, recalling its funereal origin. That crying "tree" was banked with the best gifts we could manage, and I recall my delight with a glamorous milk glass flower pot filled with bath salts topped by a shiny and unnatural blue poinsettia.

In town, I could not go to the barn to listen to the animals talking, but I thought of them and wondered what they would say.

Many years later when I had children of my own, we were horse-sitting for my in-laws in Davenport at Christmas, and I was the last one up, filling stockings. As midnight struck with Westminster chimes, I considered going to the stable. I even reached for my coat, but I hung it up again. Mute horses would have stolen something precious from me. This dearest Christmas fancy of an Iowa child was something I wanted to keep, and I have. Surely the miraculous reason for Christmas can support this endearing lesser miracle.

Celebrating in the Early 1900s

By Marie Elisabath Valborg Jørgensen, 91, as told to her daughter, Ingrid Marie Christiansen

I was born March 26, 1902, the youngest girl in a family of nine children. I grew up in the Amager section of Copenhagen, where my father, Fabrikant Frederick O. Jørgensen, owned a small metal factory and foundry. In the early 1900s, Amager was still semi-rural with many old family *gaarde* (farms). Under the supervision of my sister, Ellen, I was allowed to help make ornaments—cone-shaped *kræmmerhuse, muffer,* and woven hearts, and chains of inter-linked circles made of glued strips of glazed colored paper. On Christmas Eve, they would be used to decorate the tree along with strings of small paper Danish flags and candles in clip-on holders. Raisins, nuts, fruits, and candy filled the cones and hearts.

In late afternoon on December 24, the family members dressed in their best clothes and gathered in the dining room where the table was decked with a gleaming white linen tablecloth and napkins, fine china, crystal, and silver. Candles were lighted in the brass candlesticks that had been made in father's foundry. Mother had prepared roast goose stuffed with apples and prunes, browned potatoes, gravy, red cabbage, and red currant jelly. Wine flowed freely and many toasts were drunk. *Kransekage* and *Ris* (rice) *à l'amande* were served for dessert. Concealed in the rice was an almond, and the one who got it won a prize, a marzipan *gris* (pig). The winner teased the others by keeping the almond under the tongue while they ate more and more rice in hopes of finding the elusive almond.

After dinner, father would disappear behind the sliding door leading into the parlor. I and my little brother Christian would lie on the floor in a vain attempt to see *julenisserne.* When the door was opened, we children saw for the first time the decorated Christmas tree glowing with lighted candles. The family walked around the tree singing the traditional Danish Christmas songs: *"Julen har bragt velsignet bud,"* *"Det kimer nu til Julefest,"* *"Her kommer Jesus dine smaa,"* and *"Glade Jul, dejlige Jul,"* until father said it was time for a rousing *"Højt fra traets grønne top."* Then he distributed the beautifully wrapped presents. After the excitement over the presents had passed, my brothers played Christmas music. Robert played the violin, Torbald the clarinet, and Axel the cello. After I studied piano, I accompanied them.

My favorite presents were my dolls, Emil and Valborg. I received Valborg from the foreman in father's factory. I named her Valborg after mother's sister, for whom I received one of my own middle names. The Christmas after my little brother Christian died, father gave me an expensive boy doll with brown eyes, like Christian's, dressed in a red knitted suit similar to the one my brother had worn. I named him Emil, which was Christian's middle name. In some mysterious way, Emil was a comfort to me then and is to this day. After the death of my brother, a very small Christmas tree was set up in the kitchen on December 23, Little Christmas. I and my older brother, Frederick, each holding an arm of Christian's teddy bear and one of my dolls, danced around it. For several years, a small Christmas tree was put on Christian's grave in Sundby Kirkegaard.

On first and second Christmas Days (December 25 and 26), people visited different sets of relatives. December 25 was another day of feasting with relatives. Mother prepared what in Denmark is now known as *det store kolde bord,* a seemingly endless array of dishes beginning with oysters, raw and smoked, and continuing with smoked, spiced, and cooked eel, herring, and mackerel. Next came the meat courses including homemade *leverpostej* and many other delicious things. Uncles, aunts, and cousins came to eat and drink and make merry. On December 26, the dinner party was followed by a dance.

Today I go to church every Sunday, but in those days we did not go to church. Father was not a religious man. The only times he went to church was for a baptism, confirmation, marriage, or burial. He was typical of many Danes who happily observed the old holidays in non-religious ways. Once I begged Mother to take me to a midnight Christmas Eve service. The parish church was lit with many candles and filled with parishioners. One lady was wearing an awful-smelling perfume, and all of a sudden I fainted and had to be carried out. After that episode, my weary mother said, "you won't get me to go to another midnight service."

Early in the morning of December 31, my mother made many *æbleskiver* (similar to a waffle, sometimes with a piece of apple in the dough). Tables, covered with white tablecloths, were set up in the factory, and the workers were served *æbleskiver* and wine before the factory closed early for the holiday.

New Year's Eve was celebrated at home with a big dinner and rum pudding for dessert. At every place setting was a *knallert,* a device with two "handles" at each end. When the *knallert* was pulled apart, it made a loud noise, which I dreaded. After dinner, the dining room was cleared of furniture and the family and the guests danced to *Les Lanciers, Francais, Rits Rats, Skomagerdans, Den Svenske Maskerade, Rheinlaender polka, vals,* and other popular dances. A young woman played piano and her brother played violin. At midnight, everyone went out on the balcony to hear the chimes in *Raadhuset* (the City Hall) ring in the new year and to watch the fireworks exploding over Tivoli. Fireworks were also set off in the factory yard. A particularly noisy one, *kanonslag* (the cannon ball), climaxed the evening.

On New Year's Day everyone slept late except my mother and my sister, who prepared yet another huge dinner of all kinds of seafood, meats, and cheeses. I took advantage of these times, when there was no company, to play with dolls and doll house and later, after I had started school, to read my new books and practice the piano, which was in the dining room.

Holy Three Kings Night, January 6, which marked the end of the Christmas and New Year celebrations, was another occasion to celebrate with a dinner party and dancing. Pheasant was my father's bird of choice.

Before the beginning of Lent, we celebrated *Fastelavn.* A barrel filled with nuts, fruit, and candy was hoisted upon a scaffold in the factory yard. The men, dressed in costumes and masks, used staves to break open the barrel dangling overhead. This old custom was known as *slaa katten af tønden.* My brother Frederick injured his hand when his mask fell down over his eyes as he tried to steady the barrel with one hand while hitting a mighty blow with the other hand. Women were not allowed to participate in this sport, but one year my sister Ellen, dressed as a ragamuffin, slipped into the yard. Father shouted, "Throw the bum out!" Ellen quickly whispered to the workmen her real identity and was allowed to try her luck at smashing the barrel.

The year my birthdays was on Easter Sunday, I received so many *Paaske* (Easter) eggs that I could have opened a store. I especially liked the exquisite sugar eggs with a window in one end through which could be viewed beautiful scenes, and the decorated chocolate eggs filled with candy.

Before Easter, it was the custom to hard-boil many eggs and dye them. I remember sticking pins in both ends of a raw egg and blowing out the contents. At breakfast I placed the egg in my father's egg cup, and he pretended to be shocked when he whacked the top off the egg with his knife and found it to be empty. Eggs were eaten on Good Friday, and pancakes were served on Thursday as a concession to fasting.

In June, Midsummer, the summer solstice, longest day of the year, is celebrated on the eve of Saint Hans' (John the Baptist's) Day. My family went to *Dyrehaven* to attend an outdoor performance of the Danish operetta, *Der Var Engang.* Hundreds of people strolled from the streetcar stop in Klampenborg to the park. Those who could afford it rode in elegant carriages. I loved especially to see the ballet dancers from the *Kongelige Teater* (Theater), dressed in white ballet dresses, come dancing down from the crest of the hill, as *Elverpiger* (Fairies). Johannes Paulsen sang the stirring *Midsommervisen,* which beings with the lines, *"Vi elsker vort land."* (We love our country). In the finale, the famous Paul Reumert appeared as King Christian IV. After the show, a huge bonfire was lit and the witch on top flew with the sparks to *Bloksbjerg.*

Have a (Christmas) Heart

A Danish Christmas decoration, the interwoven paper heart, is peculiar to Denmark. The traditional Danish heart is red and white, the colors of the flag. These drawings reveal the secret of a most important manufacturing process in Danish homes before Christmas: making paper hearts for your Christmas tree!

1. You require two pieces of glazed paper, three times as long as they are wide, each a different color. The folding and cutting instructions are the same for both pieces. Fold each piece in half (see drawing), colored side out. From the fold upward, mark off a square (shown as broken line).

2. Taking the top of the square as the diameter, draw a semi-circle above the square with a compass or by means of something circular (a drinking glass or cup). Trim around the semi-circle, discarding the triangular portions.

3. In the two folded pieces of paper, cut from the exact middle of the fold up to the top edge of the square.

4. and 5. Slide the flap marked 'x' through between the doubled paper at 'o.'

6. Pull flap 'x' through and—gently—hook it over the unused flap on

the left-hand half of the heart. The other flap is now hooked over the flap marked 'o,' and slid between the parts of the second flap on the left-hand half of the heart.

7. The heart is now finished—and should be fitted with a paper handle.

8. and 9. A slightly more complicated heart can be made by cutting twice in from the fold, an equal distance apart. First you weave one flap: Hook over, in between, hook over. Then the second: In between, hook over, in between. The third flap is woven in the same way as the first.

10. Add a handle.

11. to 15. You can vary the appearance by making 4 or 6 flaps, or with a wide central flap and two narrow outer flaps, or vice versa.

—Marie Louise Paludan

A Danish Christmas Song
"Højt fra Traeets Grønne Top"

"Højt fra Traeets Grønne Top," words by P. Faber and music by E. Horne-man (1848), describes a little drama taking place on Christmas Eve. While the fiddler plays, father and children walk around the tree, decorated with candles and paper hearts and cones filled with raisins, nuts, fruits, and candy.

The narrator/father speaks to each child as he distributes presents to Signe, Peter, Anna, Henrik, William, Lotte, and Hanne. Finally, he says that mother, who is in the kitchen, will get a purse of money. The song concludes with the familiar lines, *"Julen varer laenge, koster mange Penge,"* which translates into "Christmas lasts a long time [and] costs a lot of money."

"Højt fra Traeets Grønne Top"

Verse 1

High from the tree's green top, beams the Christmas radiance.
Fiddler, play a lively tune, now begins the dancing,
Put your pretty little hand in mine; do not touch the raisins.
First the tree is shown; later it is "eaten."

Verse 2

Yes, my children, you're doing fine; You know how to trudge.
Let little Signe get her present now.
Just undo the red ribbon by yourself. How your hand is shaking.
If you tighten the string, you will choke the baby.

Verse 3

Peter likes the branch, on which the drum is hanging.
Every time he comes near it, he won't go any further.
What you wish for, you will get,
If I can trust that you won't drum before my song is finished.

Verse 4

Anna won't be content, until she gets her package,
Four Merino sheepskins, for her winter coat.
Child, you're getting too costly for me, but as you sew so neatly,
We save money anyway. Isn't that right, my daughter?

Verse 5

This banner, new and fine, I will give to Henrik.
You are strong and you are brave, you shall be our flag carrier.
How boldly he swings the flag! Children, you owe him respect.
Know that it is an honor, to carry *Dannebrog.*

Verse 6

The tree's very best treasure shall my William have;
On the shiny gold paper, you are allowed to gnaw.
Be careful, pay attention! Something is laid inside
Which you must not squeeze. It is for your nanny.

Verse 7

Oh, how soft and cozy, is that splendid hat.
It will protect grandfather from frost, and from a cold in the head.
Lotte, she can be proud, I think, she had held the yarn,
which Hanne cannot do, while she knits.

Verse 8

Children, I am getting tired; you will not get anything more.
Mother is in the kitchen, and now she deserves a treat.
She shall get this purse. Try to lift it, how heavy it is.
Christmas lasts a long time and costs much money.

Festivals in America

The *Dannebrog* flies high, music fills the air, and Americans happily consume *æbleskiver* at Danish-American festivals. The annual Tivoli Fest on

Joan Liffring-Zug Bourret photo

Folk dancers at a festival in Elk Horn, Iowa

Memorial Day weekend at Elk Horn, Iowa, the home of the Museum of Danish America, began as a community picnic to celebrate *Grundlovsdag* June 5. The population of the tiny town swells by thousands for the celebration, which includes a parade, Danish foods, performances, craft booths, a dance, and street entertainment. A Tivoli Fest king and queen are crowned. A storyteller, folk dancers, and the Tivoli Choraliers may perform, and visitors can tour the 1848 authentic Danish Windmill.

On the first weekend after Thanksgiving, Elk Horn and Kimballton sponsor a Julfest for Christmas.

Danish Days in Solvang, California, are Friday through Sunday the third weekend in September. A Danish Days maid is selected. Attractions include gymnastics, accordion and oompah music, Danish dancing, and storytelling. There are demonstrations of crafts, lace-making, figurine painting, and rosemaling. The Saturday parade is for everyone. Sunday's parade is devoted to children. The dinner dance Saturday night features a smorgasbord. Other offerings may be a musical at the Terrace Theater and an organ concert of the works of Danish composers.

The non-stop Danish excitement on the third weekend in August in Greenville, Michigan, has been going on each year since 1965. The first festival was so successful that it stretched to three days of parades, music, arts and crafts, Danish food, downtown street stands, window displays, dramatic productions, fireworks, and the crowning of Miss Danish Festival.

The "Danish capital of Nebraska" sets its festival as close as possible to June 5, the Danish Constitution Day. Dannebrog is noted for its beautiful Danish-style architecture, including symmetrical facades with peaked dormers above the doorways, and windows on either side. West of Omaha and Lincoln, Dannebrog is a short drive north and west from Interstate 80 and Grand Island.

Viborg, South Dakota, celebrates Danish Days the first week in June as brightly costumed Danish dancers perform in the streets and Danish delicacies are served with flair. Viborg also has hosted the South Dakota State Pork Show for more then a quarter of a century. The Red River Danes, organized to "keep alive an appreciation of Danish culture, traditions, and fellowship," draw members from a 100-mile radius of Fargo, North Dakota, and Moorhead, Minnesota. The group meets the last Monday night of every month and participates in the Scandinavian *Hjemkomst* Festival in Fargo-Moorhead the last weekend in June.

Tyler, Minnesota, is host to *Æbleskiver* Days, typically held in July. In 2012, the festival included a 5K and eight-mile run/bike, a golf tournament, model airplane demonstrations, a talent show, street dancing, and even a beard contest. Plenty of delicious Danish food is offered, including, of course, plenty of *æbleskiver!* The Danish American Center at 4200 Cedar Avenue in Minneapolis schedules monthly evening folk meetings, noon dinners by a Danish chef on Wednesdays and Sundays, evening lectures, a children's Danish dance group, and an adult Danish dance group, and other activities including a large summer picnic and a Christmastime dinner and dance at a hotel. The Center's Fellowship manages the Danish section of the Festival of Nations, a multi-cultural event held in downtown St. Paul each year in the spring. Danish Day is celebrated in Minneapolis on the Sunday nearest Danish Constitution Day, June 5.

National Dress: A Lively Misnomer

By Minna Kragelund for the Press and Cultural Relations Department of the Ministry of Foreign Affairs of Denmark

Museums are always pressed to exhibit old Danish national costumes. The garments are so beautifully made and so richly colored that they are clearly distinguishable from present-day clothing. However, "national dress" is a misnomer because there was no single type of costume worn all over Denmark. One of the main features of peasant costumes of the eighteenth and nineteenth centuries was their individual character.

For about 150 years, from about 1750 to 1900, the peasant costume had the form familiar to us today from painting and genre scenes of everyday life during those years. Much of the clothing was partially homemade. "Home-woven" did not necessarily mean the fabric was woven at home, merely that the yarn had been spun at home from wool or flax which the peasant and his wife and helpers had harvested.

Before enclosure of common land in about 1800, most Danes lived in village communities, with farmholdings built close together. The people lived closely and were socially dependent on one another. When a new cottage needed building or plastering with mud, or when wool had to be carded and spun, the young folk from the village would assemble and help in the work, and the woman of the house would supply food and drink for her "guests." This mutual aid system also worked well in times of illness or accident.

In such societies, three generations frequently lived under the same roof. The grandparents took on the status of pensioners but still lent a hand in everyday life, grandmother perhaps minding the children as she turned the spinning wheel. Men and women had a sharp division of labor. The man's domain was the field and the livestock; the woman's was indoor work, milking, and poultry. Indoor work was more than merely cooking and cleaning. More important was the manufacture of various fabrics and garments, not only for family members, but also for the servants, whose payment might consist in part of an agreed length of woolen or linen cloth. And the domestic servants probably had a corner of the flax field as their own, having a week off to return to their parents' home to prepare flax for weaving.

Today we generally marry because of mutual feelings, but in those days, marriage was an economic relationship between two families. There was no "safety net" to catch the socially deprived, and it was essential to secure a decent future for your offspring, which meant ensuring their economic prospects. The farsighted mother began work on her daughter's trousseau while the child was still young. This increased the girl's assets and thereby her marital chances. And what mother did not have higher hopes for her daughter than she herself had fulfilled? The aim was to improve the daughter's social potential.

If a girl, despite all these preparations, failed to marry, she could face a miserable future. The spinster had virtually no place in a society that was based on complete, almost self-sufficient families. The unmarried woman could perhaps work at home as a domestic servant or become a weaver or spinner or seamstress. Some became private tutors, but these girls came usually from higher social strata than the peasantry.

Roughly speaking, a girl aimed to have three types of woven fabric in her hope chest. This receptacle stood in the main room of the cottage, and it was customary for female visitors to be invited to admire the contents of the chest. Each daughter preferably had her own chest. In southern Jutland, adjacent to the German border, people took pride in showing off their possessions, and there are examples of hope chests standing not only along the parlor walls but also lined up for instant inspection in the middle of the floor! The three woven fabrics a girl simply "must" have were fustian and ticking for bed linen, frieze and linsey-woolsey for garment-making, and linen (for shirts and shifts), and, in certain parts of the country, decorative pieces to be hung on the walls on festive occasions. For the most part, garments were of woolen fabric made by the woman herself or by the professional weaver. The peasantry had only a limited range of colors to draw from but they mastered the art of combining the various possibilities with immense inventiveness. Many patterns appear virtually all over the country and there were innumerable variations in the use of the stripe.

Every smallholding had at least a few sheep because clothing was something you produced yourself, and the woolen variety could be made at home from start to finish. Wool was carded, spun, and perhaps dyed at home with boiled vegetable coloring. The latter process might, however, be delegated to the professional dyer in town, who could also be relied upon to dye finished knitwear or handprint linen items with patterned blocks.

In women's Sunday best we see most readily the distinction between various regions, and the most obvious differences were in the arrangement and composition of the headdress. Women always wore some form of headgear—either a bonnet or a scarf. The black bonnet was a sign of the woman's dignity, showing that she had honored society's expectations, having married and set up a family. Great ingenuity was exhibited in ornamentation of the headpiece. It frequently was made up of a number of items—the bonnet, the piece of linen underneath, and the scarf holding the whole assembly in place. The latter might be in broad lace or finely embroidered tulle, showing the economic standing of the wearer, or rather, the economic standing of her husband. The same applied to bonnet embroidery.

The island of Zealand had a tradition for trimming bonnets with embroidery in gold and silver thread. Not only was there a difference in what the smallholder's wife and farmer's wife might wear, there was also a difference in which bonnets ladies might be seen wearing on which occasions. A gold neckpiece was, of course, the finest of all.

Women's costumes were made up of a variety of parts that could be combined in many ways. Petticoats were worn by the layer, and were long. Only the foot was free. Underneath, the women wore a shift but no knickers or bloomers. In rural communities, knickers or bloomers were not used until the end of the nineteenth century. She wore an apron whatever the occasion—kitchen chores or family festivities. It might be of fine silk or embroidered mull. The upper part of the body was covered by a fabric jacket or blouse (occasionally this was knitted).

In some localities it was also the custom to wear a close-fitting bodice-piece fastened by hooks or laced at the front. The bodice, jacket, and petticoats were almost invariably edged and decorated with silk tape, flat or patterned. It was considered indecent to reveal the shoulders and throat, so women wore one or more light scarves about their necks, usually held in place by pins.

The minor parts of the costume were bought at the door from peddlers or in the nearest town. In those days the law prohibited the setting up of shops in rural districts. The wool merchants in the area around Herning were one of the few exceptions. They were expressly authorized to travel around the country selling woolen knitwear made in the Herning district of Jutland.

The male dress was fairly simple and, like that of the women, was made mainly of flax and wool—materials that the country people could produce themselves. Men of the period wore knee breeches, usually of leather, which was a highly practical material and also available on the farm. The breeches were windproof, and would stretch slightly as the men went about their field work.

Men did not wear underpants either, resorting instead to stuffing their long shirts well into their trousers. They normally wore home-knitted white woolen stockings reaching up above the knee and held (either above or below the knee) by a garter ribbon.

It was quite customary for men to wear several jerseys and jackets. They might well be made of the same fabric. In front they displayed a row of buttons, and if they man was fairly well-off or had inherited them from a rich relative, the buttons might be of silver. Most often they were of tin or some other metal. Horn buttons were common, too.

Like their womenfolk, men always wore some kind of headgear. This was partly traditional, but it was also because of the poor quality of contemporary housing; invariably a draft whistled through the house. To safeguard health you kept your head warm.

Men wore knitted "nightcaps," either a natural brown or red in color. The cap was double, the outer piece being long and carrying a tassel, the inner piece fitting the wearer's head neatly and bearing loop-stitching or other open-work to improve its warmth-giving qualities. For finer occasions a man might wear a tall black top hat over his nightcap.

In everyday life, men and women both wore clogs. They were inexpensive and lasted a long time, although they could be uncomfortable. Men often had a long leather top-boot for better occasions, and both sexes wore a dress shoe of leather with a buckle in front. When invited to a dance or other celebration at a neighboring farm, the custom was for the guests to wear clogs as far as the courtyard and to switch into shoes just before entering the house. You had to take good care of the shoes; they probably were the only pair of shoes you would ever have.

Every celebration or festive occasion called for a dance. Often many people were packed into the farmhouse, but they all managed to dance at the same time since many dances were chain dances or done in strict rotation, one couple with the next. Everyone knew the direction in which they were to move, so dancing did not need the same space as twentieth-century rock-n-roll! The traditional national costumes began dying out in the mid-nineteenth century, and with them the old dances also began to disappear. They were closely associated with the special form of country music played on the violin.

Around the turn of the century, a number of groups were set up in Denmark to revive the old country culture. Initially, the music and dance were the attractions, but these led naturally to an interest in national costumes. The dancers jigged and swayed to the old country music in copies of the old costumes.

Landsforeningen Danske Folkedanseres og Spillemand (the Danish Country Dancing Society) was set up in Copenhagen in 1901, the first formal move to give folk dancing an official status. Local dancing societies later sprang up around the country. Today Denmark has about 15,000 regular folk-dancers, forming a federation through their 140 local societies. Courses are arranged in music, dancing, and dressmaking, and folk dancers from many countries take part in rallies and conferences.

Some folk dancers approach their subject with deep cultural interest, making a thorough study of the historical background to the old peasant life-style and folk-dancing movement. Others treat folk dancing as an enjoyable hobby, meeting like-minded friends in a light-hearted atmosphere and at the same time getting much healthful exercise. Members of both groups may invest in a costume that can cost between 5–10,000 Danish kroner. Many of the materials for the new copies have been produced specially by people who have studied the old items in museums and in private collections, which creates a firm link between Denmark's ancient peasant culture and today's industrial society.

A Danish American Discovers Danish Folk Dancing in Denmark

By Ingrid Marie Christiansen

Where I grew up in rural Illinois, there was no Scandinavian community. For many years I harbored an interest in Scandinavian folk dancing, but my Danish relatives thought Danish folk dancing had disappeared in Denmark. When the well-known folk dance leader, Gordon Tracie, told me about a week-long summer course to train teachers of Danish folk dancing, I resolved to attend. I flew from the U.S.A. to Denmark, traveled by train and ferry to Funen, rode a bus to Kerteminde, walked along the dark coastal road to the folk high school, and arrived in time for the first evening dance party, or *Legestue* as it is called in Danish.

Entering the brightly lit hall, I was thrilled to see enthusiastic people dancing to the glorious music of violins, clarinet, bass, and piano. Dance leaders called out directions: *"Et chassé og gaa og gaa," "Sving egen," "Kaede."* With good dancers to guide me, I joined in on the fun. All too soon came a family waltz mixer and the final fast *hopsa,* which I danced as though I had twinkle toes. Within twenty-four hours I had finally discovered the joys of Danish folk dancing.

The course was designed to be completed in four summers. A diploma certified that a person who completed the course could teach Danish folk dancing in the public school evening programs.

Each day began with breakfast and Morning Song, followed by a class in basic steps, a required class for both dancers and musicians. Attendance slackened as the week progressed and more dancers arrived late and red-eyed. According to tradition, the avid dancers stayed up an hour later each night until the final night, when dancing lasted until breakfast. Parallel to the classes for dance teachers were classes for musicians, the youngest barely in their teens. Both groups were together for meals, evening dances, and refreshments. On Friday evenings the local community was invited to a concert given by the musicians, followed by refreshments and dancing for all. Lectures were given by specialists in Danish costume, the social history of the Danish peasants, dance history, and music theory. There were group discussions and projects. The *Aspirants,* as they were called, were assigned to teach dances to the other members of their class, who pretended not to know the dances. Only I was truly ignorant. Tactful, constructive criticism was given both by the master teacher and the class members. I was impressed by the level of professionalism and learned much from these sessions.

The summer courses gave me a marvelous introduction into Danish folk dancing. Over the years, I met people who later became important folk dance leaders of children, young people, and adult groups, and highly respected musicians. Moreover, I saw how much the Danes enjoy their music and dance and how proud they are to pass their culture on to the next generation.

A Brief History of Danish Dancing

At the turn of the century, traditional Danish folk dancing and music were disappearing rapidly with the advance of industrialism. In the early 1900s, Danish researchers, following the lead of the Swedes, went into rural communities to transcribe the music and dance. Books of dances and music from the various regions of Denmark were published. The work continues today with the interviewing, recording, and filming of venerable musicians and dancers.

Many of the Danish quadrilles danced today derive from dances in *The English Dancing Master,* by John Playford, whose first book was published in 1651. As English longways set dances were unsuitable to some small square Danish parlors, some were adapted into square sets or quadrilles. In the Danish dance tradition are dances for two, three, six, and eight couples. There are also *raekke* (contraline) dances, dances for one man and two women, dances for women only and men only, and a few old dances from the Morris tradition, which died out in Scandinavia but continues to thrive in England. When the nineteenth century polka and waltz were introduced to Scandinavia, these steps were often incorporated into existing dances. Denmark's strategic position, a peninsula separating the Baltic from the North Sea, exposed Danes to foreign influences from the continent, the British Isles, and the countries rimming the Baltic Sea.

Travelers, professional soldiers and sailors, brought back music and dance from the Rhinelands, France, England, Scotland, Spain, and other countries. The Danes happily adapted everything to suit their own taste. To this day, Danes are eager to learn the latest dances. But what about dancing before the 1650s? The *kaede* (chain) dance, with vague similarities to the twentieth-century bunny hop, was the popular dance of the Middle Ages. It nearly disappeared in Denmark but continues to flourish in the Faeroe Islands. Fortunately, texts of the Danish medieval ballads and some of the music survived, thanks to the efforts of N.F.S. Grundtvig. Apart from their literary value, the old ballads are a valuable source of information about social life in the Middle Ages. In the eighteenth century the minuet was a popular dance and is still danced as a folk dance in Denmark. Only the splendid music for the *proportion* and *serras* survived—in notebooks such as Rasmus Storm's, circa 1760. However, on the island of Fanø off the coast of Denmark, the *Fannik* and *Sønderhoning* and *rask* are still danced in a tradition for more than 200 years.

Danish Folk Dance Music and Folk Instruments

Danish folk dance is happy-sounding music. Tunes in minor keys are rare. Dancing is associated with happy times. Holidays and special family events such as marriages and anniversaries were celebrated with a *fest* (party) that included good food, drinks, singing, speeches, and dancing. A *spillemand* (musician) was usually hired for the occasion, and people who could not afford to hire one sang for the dancing. Sometimes the tunes had verses, but other times people sang nonsense syllables such as *attengulerødder* (eighteen carrots) or "tra-la-la."

In earlier times, few *spillemaend* received any formal musical training. Often they came from musical families whose members supplemented their incomes as farmers or craftsmen by playing for dances. The son of a shoemaker, smith, or butcher learned to play the fiddle or clarinet by playing along with an older musician. After the passage of the public education act in 1814, however, many received musical training and earned their meager living as professional *spillemaend*.

The violin was the most common and best-loved folk instrument. In the Music History Museum in Copenhagen, old folk fiddles are on display, including pocket-size fiddles and one made out of a wooden shoe. The clarinet was popular. Like the violin, it was easy to transport. Svend Jørgensen, in his book, *Om spillemaend og spillemaendsmusik,* remarks that the cello and the bass fiddle were "welcomed to give bottom to the music," but that the bass fiddle was "awfully hard to transport." The recorder (an early flute) and jawharp were also played. By the 1860s, horn music had become popular. By the 1890s, according to Jørgensen, any farm boy with musical talent played the horn, or tried to, perhaps with the hope of being placed in a band if he were conscripted to become a soldier. (How my old grandfather relished his memories of playing horn in a military band!) In the 1900s, the piano was played for social dancing, especially at home. More recently the accordion has become an acceptable folk instrument and is played along with the violin, clarinet, and bass for folk dancing.

Much as Danish peasants loved to dance, there were two periods when religious fanatics, believing musicians to be in league with the devil, incited community members to hurl the violin and music notebook of the local *spillemand* into a bonfire while he and his family watched in fright and horror. The first period was during the reign of Christian VI, from 1720 to

1750, when followers of Brorson's Puritanism were convinced that music and dance were utterly sinful and had to be rooted out. More than a century later, during another wave of pietism, many who immigrated to America and Canada believed dancing to be a sin, and did not pass on to their children the old folk dances.

However, Danish folk music and dance are alive and doing very well in Denmark. Many organizations now sponsor festivals and workshops in Denmark. The Nordic nations cooperatively promote and publish dance and music research. Every three years, a festival known as *Nordlek* is held in one of the Scandinavian countries. Dancers, musicians, and singers of all ages and from all the Nordic countries gather to attend workshops, special programs, and evening dances. The event culminates in a colorful spectacle. Imagine a parade of 5,000 folk dancers and flag bearers in beautiful costumes, led by people carrying flags and banners, marching into a park or stadium to sing and perform Scandinavian folk dances. It's a sight you'll never forget.

The Danish Folk Arts

Many Americans are unaware of Denmark's rich tradition of folk arts. The tourist in Denmark is enticed to visit the big modern stores. *This Week in Copenhagen* describes things that one can buy, "from porcelain, glassware and jewelry to furniture, fashion, and children's toys." Demark is proud of its modern Danish design, and rightly so. The Danish Handcraft Guild (Vimmelskaffet 38 in the middle of Strøget), advertises that "in its dynamic workshop, embroidery patterns and knitwear are developed continuously in cooperation with technically and artistically qualified skilled craftsmen whose work can be seen in museums and at exhibitions all over the world." However, it isn't as easy for a tourist in Denmark to find objects of traditional folk design as it would be in Norway or Sweden. Only the most determined will be able to find an authentic folk costume for one's self or one's grandchild.

In contrast to the Copenhagen guide, the shopping section of *Stockholm This Week* lists Hemslojd, the Swedish Handicraft Society, which advertises "genuine Swedish handicrafts, special works from local craftsmen in wood, leather, metal, ceramics, basket making, knitting and textiles, embroidery kits, and many kinds of yarn for weaving, embroidery, and knitting, and

Swedish national dress." Hemslojd stores can be found in all the popular tourist areas of Sweden. The same is true for Norway's Husfliden stores, where one can buy trolls, sweaters, rosemaling, carved wood objects, textiles, books about the folk arts, and recordings of folk music. At Heimat in Oslo, folk dancers can conveniently order complete hand-tailored costumes, or the materials with which to make them, knitted socks, hand-woven garters, bunad jewelry, shoes with buckles, purses, hats, and other accessories. Although similar items are available in Denmark, unfortunately in takes perseverance to find them. When tourists become interested in Danish folk arts, change will undoubtedly follow demand.

How does the tourist learn about Danish folk arts? Scholars have written on all aspects of the Danish folk arts. In addition to comprehensive books about folk arts and costumes, there are books about specific areas in the folk arts. A bibliography by S. Schoubye lists books about pottery, carpentry, weaving, straw mosaic, sweetheart gifts, marriage licenses, and book markers from old psalm books. Nearly all the Danish museums and historic places sell monographs or guide books about the folk arts characteristic to their district, e.g. lace from Tønder, embroidery from Hedebo, farm furnishings on Rømø. Nevertheless, for an American who does not read Danish, it is difficult to learn, in the U.S.A., about the folk arts. The most enjoyable way to learn about the folk arts is, of course, to take a trip to Denmark and visit any of the many museums which have collections of folk arts. A museum guide is printed in *This Week Guides,* and pamphlets about Danish museums are available from any tourist information office.

What is meant by Danish folk arts? In his book *Dansk Folkekunst* (Thaning & Appels Forlag, Copenhagen, 1963), Kai Uldall distinguishes folk arts from fine arts as *"brugs kunsten,"* meaning things that were made and used by ordinary people living on farms in and small rural communities, e.g. the butcher, the baker, the candlestick maker, as opposed to fancy things used by members of the bourgeois and upper classes. He chose not to include clothing in his book. However, other scholars have written extensively about what people wore, a subject that includes not only fabrics and yarns but also lace-making, embroidery, stockings, woven garter bands, shoes, hats, gloves, buttons, jewelry, and bridal crowns. After industrialization came to Denmark and the Constitution was adopted in 1849, people had more opportunity to rise in society. Wearing store-bought clothes and using store-bought things became a way of showing off one's social status. Although people continued to make many things by hand, and still do, by 1875 the era of the folk arts was essentially over.

Thus, peasant furniture, for instance—once seen in homes—is now commonly seen in Danish museums. Before the era of chimneys, when the smoke went up and out a hole in the roof, most wood objects were carved but not painted, as smoke would have discolored the paint. After chimneys became common, it became popular to decorate household things with paint. The furniture, walls, and even the ceilings and floors were painted. The motifs for decorations varied. In North Jutland, where there was much trade with Norway, flowers were painted on the walls and door panels, chests, and wooden things such as tankards and boxes, revealing the influence of Norwegian rosemaling. In southern Jutland, the influences came mostly from Friesland and Holland. In coastal towns, where men had been to sea, it was not unusual for a panel in a cupboard to be painted with a scene from Barbados or some other exotic port. Before the Reformation (1536), artisans found inspiration in church from fresco wall paintings and stained glass windows, and later from illustrations in their family Bibles. The King's monogram was another source for decorative ideas. Objects observed in nature, flowers (tulips and daisies), trees, animals, insects, ripe grains, all were sources for designs.

Intricately carved alcove beds and four-poster beds *(himmelseng)* with richly embroidered bed linens can be found in museums. There are benches designed for different uses: a bride's bench, a folding bench, benches that fastened to walls, and benches with a drawer that pulls out to reveal a bed—the precursor of our modern sofa bed. Chairs were designed for a variety of uses. For women wearing very full skirts, there were chairs with a wide rounded back called *bøjlekringstol.* For the elderly who tend to fall asleep sitting up, there was a comfortable arm chair with cheek flaps.

The table designs are still practical, especially the folding tables. There are all sors of cupboards *(skabe)* and wall shelves. I found a prototype of one that hung in my aunt's parlor, a hanging pyramid-shaped wall shelf on which she displayed various souvenir spoons.

A *chatol* is an impressive piece of furniture that combines a chest of drawers and a cupboard with doors *(overskab)*. A magnificent *chatol* of polished mahogany dominated the wall in my *Tante* (aunt) Kirsten's parlor where the family portraits were hung on either side. Speaking of chests, my cousin salvaged an abandoned old chest in a shed on his *moster's* (mother's sister's) estate, that had been used by the young women in the family for collecting their dowries *(brude udstyr)* for at least 150 years. The giant-size chest always reminds me of the chest in Rolvaang's novel, *Giants in the*

Earth, which Beret brought with her from Norway across the ocean to a primitive homestead in South Dakota.

Danish women loved embroidery and created decorative collars centuries ago.

This is a folk art paper cut mobile by Joan Kristensen from Odense, Denmark.

From Here to Antiquity: Finding Danish Roots
What's in a Name?

Americans, content for decades to be part of the melting pot, now are eager to claim the distinction of their heritage. It always seemed that genealogical research in a nation where 60 percent of all surnames end in "sen" would be a hopeless undertaking. However, a Danish Canadian relative I didn't know found me and proved that it can be done. He shoved my mother's family back to the 1600s. Tracing your ancestry was difficult in the days when Jens, the son of Peter, became Jens Petersen and Jens's son became Peter Jensen. However, all that was ended by an 1856 government decree.

After that, all children carried the surname of their fathers. Yet in Denmark today, about half the population shares 14 names. My own maiden name, Jensen, is claimed by some 375,000 Danes, 32,000 of them living in Copenhagen. My mother had problem when she married a Jensen who was not related to her sister's husband, also named Jensen. And people have always been convinced that I must be kin to assorted unrelated Jensens. How will it all work out? Soon there will be a million Jensens with the Nielsens close behind.

My mother's maiden name was Faurschou, which seemed quite rare to us. Furthermore, we assumed that the spelling had been savaged during the immigration procedure and the final letters should have been "skov," meaning woods. However, my Canadian relative, who found me genealogically, has unearthed more than 1,800 Faurschous, and the spelling has been unchanged since the early eighteenth century at least.

The genealogy certainly has its share of "sens" names: Svenningsen, Christensen, Jensen, Mortensen, Laursen, Andersen, Ibsen, Pedersen, Jacobsen, Nielsen, Jorgensen, MiChelsen, Olesen, Rasmussen, and Karstensen are just about all the "sen" names ever heard.

One name, Duedal, derives from a place. It means "dove valley." Another non-sen name is Balling, but records show that this name's owner was also known as Jensen. The surnames of famous Danes tend to be more distinctive: Jacob Riis, Lauritz Melchior, N.S.F. Grundtvig, Jean Hersholt, Vitus Bering, Victor Borge, Kaj Munk, Niels Bohr, Tycho Brahe, and Soren Kierkegaard. But how much more famous can anyone be than Hans Christian Andersen?

The largest proportion of Danish immigrants came to this country relatively late, so family memories and records hopefully may solve the American part of the search.

Denmark, Norway, and Sweden were once united and Germany controlled Slesvig from 1864 to 1920. That makes a difference in the kind of records one can find. Many Danish parish records were kept haphazardly before 1814, when uniform printed books were issued to get the same information from all parishes. For registers in the Lutheran National Church and all other Danish denominations, the best source is the Danish provincial archives (Landsarkivet). Some parish registers go back to 1660.

Note: These addresses are for in person visits only, not mail requests.

In Sjælland, the address is:
Landsarkivet
Jagtvej 10, DK-2200
Copenhagen N, Denmark
If your family came from Fyn
    write:
Landsarkivet for Fyn
Jernbanegade 36A
DK-5000 Odense C, Denmark

The Nørrejylland address is:
Landsarkivet
Lille Sankt Hansgade 5
DK-8800, Viborg, Denmark
For de Sønderjyske
Landsdele, apply to:
Landsarkivet
Haderslevvej 45
DK-6200, Aabenraa, Denmark

Census records are kept by:
The Danish National Archives (Rigsarkivet)
States Arkiver Sekretariatet
Rigsdagsgården 9
DK-1218
Copenhagen K, Denmark

The forms date from 1787, and those from 1845 onward contain information on birthplaces.

The National Archives also keeps military records. The draft register dates back to 1788, when all the sons of peasants were registered for the draft at birth.

Property records may be found at the Landsarkiv (regional archives). Land registers with information about tenants go back to the early 1700s. The regional archives also keep the burgess rolls of towns in their area, and they contain professional information and descending genealogy of citizens.

The Danes Worldwide Archives *(Udvandrerarkivet)* has copies of the original emigration lists compiled by the police from 1868 to 1940, including name, birthplace, age, and destination of the emigrant. Records are in chronological order, so it is important to have an approximate year of emigration. The collection includes letters, postcards, diaries, photographs, and portraits. Write to:

Ved Vor Frue Kirke
P. O. Box 1731
9100 Aalborg, Denmark

The Ministry of Foreign Affairs fact sheet Tracing Your Danish Ancestors and Relatives is available from these two sources and online below:

The Royal Danish Embassy   Landsarkivet for Sjaelland m. m.
3200 Whitehaven Street   N. W. Postbox 661, Jagtvej 10
Washington, D.C. 20008-3683   DK-2200 Copenhagen N

http://usa.um.dk/en/about-denmark/tracing-your-danish-ancestors/

The fact sheet of the Ministry of Foreign Affairs states:

"First, the handwriting commonly used in Denmark until about 1900 was the old Gothic script. Consequently this handwriting appears in all the old documents."

"Second, as late as 1850 the majority of the rural population did not use a permanent family name; instead, the sons used their father's given name plus sen (English, son) while the daughters added *datter* (Enlish, daughter). Thus Peter Olsen's son would be Ole Petersen and the daughter might be Karen Petersdatter."

"Another difficulty arose when many names underwent changes after emigration; thus Jorgensen and Johansen and Jensen might all have been changed into Johnson."

The name and age or birthdate of the person is helpful, "but above all the birthplace is of importance. If this is not possible to find, the last permanent address in Denmark may be of help either the town or parish in which registration took place."

Other sources that could be helpful are:

1. Oral or written information the family can supply, such as old stories.

2. Conduct books: "From 1832 and well into the twentieth century all Danish domestics were required to possess conduct books in which comments on their conduct could be made by their employers. The fly-leaf usually bears valuable information about birth date and home parish."

3. Letters from Denmark: "Old letters from Danish relatives may still be available, and return addresses, maybe even postmarks, may be extremely helpful in suggesting the best starting point for an investigation."

4. Books and documents brought along from Denmark "may be in the form of diaries or a family Bible containing entries about memorable events in the family. There may also be draft papers or service records whose almost unintelligible abbreviations may lead to new openings."

5. "Photos brought along or sent over by relatives left behind can also give clues; for example, the name of the photographer could be a clue. It is important that such material not be destroyed; if the family does not want to keep it, the Danes Worldwide Archives will be happy to receive the material."

6. "Naturalization documents of the immigrant generation usually state when and where the immigration took place, and may lead to the relevant official records. The same holds true for wills, social benefit applications, deeds, etc."

7. "The United States National Archives, Washington, D. C., contain an almost inexhaustible amount of source material such as passenger manifests, census records, military records, and naturalization records."

8. "Thanks to the Genealogical Society of the Church of Jesus Christ of the Latter-Day Saints, 50 East North Temple, Salt Lake City, Utah 84150, many original Danish records are on microfilm, available to the public at the church's Salt Lake City library's branch libraries, free of charge. Names of researchers accredited in Danish research, who will, for a fee, carry out the research required, are available."

9. The Genealogical Society published *A Genealogical Guidebook and Atlas of Denmark,* edited by Frank Smith and Finn A. Thomsen. It is out of print but possibly can be found in libraries.

Paper cuttings by Hans Christian Andersen

Holding the Heritage Fast and Costumes

There are many small ways to reach "across oceans, across time" to pass the heritage on to later generations.

You can do it with food, making the dishes that grandparents and great-grandparents relished. You can do it in the home, adding Danish touches like the blue and white Christmas plates and using the Danish national colors, red and white.

You can do it in the way you keep Christmas—making woven hearts for the tree, putting a sheaf of grain out for the birds, hiding a lucky almond in the rice pudding, adding *nisser* (elves in pointed caps) to the holiday decor to ensure a happy Christmas.

You can do it by reading periodicals like *The Danish Pioneer (Den Danske Pioneer)*, published in Hoffman Estates, Illinois, and online at: www.dendanskepioneer.com, and *The Bee (Bien)*, the Danish bi-weekly newspaper published in Porter Ranch, California, and for contact information online visit: www.biendk.com.

You can do it by considering the folk wisdom of the Danes in their proverbs. A few of these:

"Better thin beer than an empty jug."
"The horse one cannot have has every fault."
"Gifts should be handed, not hurled."
"Hope is the dream of waking."
"You may light another's candle at your own without loss."
"When there is room in the heart, there is room in the house."

The *Danish Literary Magazine* is published online free twice a year as a means to inform foreign publishers, literary agents, and translators about trends in Danish literature. You can vist the publication at:

http://www.kunst.dk/english/initiatives/danish-literary-magazine/

You can seek out fellowship in the Danish Brotherhood or Danish

Sisterhood. The Danish Brotherhood in America was formed in 1882, an outgrowth of *Danske Vaabenbrodre* (Danish Brothers in Arms). Besides kindred feeling, the Brotherhood offers death benefits and retirement benefits. Membership was opened to women in 1961. A national headquarters building of typical Danish architecture was built in 1967 at Omaha, Nebraska.

Through its local lodges, the Brotherhood sponsors lectures, educational programs, workshops, and Commuity Danish Days to keep the heritage alive. It contributes to projects such as the archway entrance to the Hans Christian Andersen Park in California. It donates to flood victims, and helps support five Danish Homes for the Aged established by local lodges. National scholarships and camp grants are available to insured members. Brotherhood lodges are numbered from one, in Omaha, to 350, in the Albany-Corvallis-Lebanon area of Oregon. In 2010, the brotherhood had about 8,000 members.

The Danish Sisterhood of America was organized in 1883 at Negaunee, Michigan. There are forty-six lodges across the United States, Ontario, and British Columbia, Canada. My lodge is No. 3, organized in 1884 in Davenport, Iowa. The red satin banner adorned with the heart-centered shield marks our meeting place. We answer roll call with a Danish word. It is usually laughably pronounced. We *le, tale,* and *spise,* (laugh, talk, and eat). We provide a touch of Danish Christmas for a festival of trees. We display our Danish treasures at culture fests, and we enjoy programs about trips to the homeland. Each meeting reinforces our identity as Danish Americans. Each month we receive the *Danish Sisterhood News,* which offers recipes, ads for Danish goods and travel, and news and information from the lodges.

We have a royal sister in Queen Margrethe of Denmark, who was made an honorary member of the Supreme Lodge when she and Prince Henrik came to the United States during its bicentennial celebrations.

What can you do to claim your heritage? Try the library, the chamber of commerce, or the newspaper for information on the Sisterhood. To help preserve the rich story of the Danish experience in America, you can become a member of the Museum of Danish America. Contact the museum online at www.dkmuseum.org or visit at 2212 Washington Street, Elk Horn, Iowa.

You may want a Danish costume for festivals and special events. Clothing typical of the regions was worn well into the nineteenth century in

Denmark. Beautifully decorated woolen garments are expensive, however, and may be too heavy for American summer festivals. One option is to find a picture and an accomplished seamstress to translate it into something wearable. Members of my Danish Sisterhood lodge got together for a sewing bee and made mine, copying the garb of a costumed doll. You may not like the style of your place of origin, and in that case, why not borrow a feature or two from somewhere else? Most of the bonnets I saw were too deep for comfort, so I simply narrowed the brim. Almost all of the district costumes feature a long skirt with an easy flow, and a decorative apron that falls between six and twelve inches above the skirt hem. In America, the look is completed with a white blouse and a bonnet as simple or elaborate as you want to make it. If you can manage some *Hedebo* embroidery or *Tønder* lace to see it off, so much the better.

Men can achieve the Danish look with knee breeches, long socks, a vest in a pattern or red, and a cap with a tassel.

Claiming and maintaining the Danish heritage may take a bit of effort, but as the Danish proverb says, "God gives every bird its food but does not drop it into the nest." So let birds of a Danish feather flock together!

The Danish Folk Dancers of Los Angeles danced at the opening ceremonies of the 1984 Olympics in Los Angeles. Since the 1950s, they have performed in Los Angeles for the visit of Queen Margrethe II, Southern California, Solvang, and Disneyland.

The sketches above and at left, by Joyce Gribsov of Bend, Oregon, show authentic Danish costumes. They are patterned after historic ones found in museums.

The Dagmar Cross

Today, Denmark is mostly Lutheran. However, prior to the Reformation, it was mostly Catholic.

In the year 1186, Queen Dagmar was born a princess in Bohemia. Later, she became the wife of the Danish King, Valdemar II, who was king during the years 1202–1241.

When Queen Dagmar gave birth to her second son in 1213, she died. In 1690, her grave was opened and she was wearing a cross that was thought to date back to the year 1000. On one side of the Dagmar cross a crucifix was displayed and on the other side of the cross, Jesus was in the center and starting at the right hand side was St. John the Evangelist, at the bottom was St. Basil, at the left was Our Lady, and at the top was St. John Chrysostom.

Queen Dagmar was buried at St. Bendt's (Benedict's) Church in Ringsted, Denmark next to her husband, Kind Valdemar II.

Food, Glorious Food

The near hush that falls over a Danish gathering when dinner is served characterizes people with an intense appreciation of good food giving their full attention to savoring it. Only after dessert and coffee will conversation fully resume. And speaking of dessert, a meal without one is, to a Dane, like a love affair with no kisses.

Most Danish Americans learned how to love the best-known national dishes at such an early age that we attached no nationality to them, but now we know. We prize the heritage recipes that preserve our Danishness.

Recipe Contents

Appetizers

The traditional Danish "cold table" is paradise for those who love cocktail party nibbling, but its name is misleading. Hot dishes frequently are found on a "cold table," as well as the glorious lineup of Danish cheeses and *smørrebrød* miniatures. Beautiful tidbits are the real works of art, and the dips are divine.

Summer Sausage
Spegepølse

Lois Peterson, Danish Sisterhood Lodge #3, Davenport, Iowa

- 4 pounds lean ground beef
- 4 tablespoons liquid smoke
- 4 tablespoons Morton's Tender Quick® salt
- 1 teaspoon garlic powder
- 1 teaspoon onion powder
- 1 teaspoon coarsely ground pepper
- 1 cup cold water

Mix and form into several rolls of any size preferred. Wrap each in foil and refrigerate for 24 hours. Leave in foil and cover with cold water. Bring to a boil and simmer for one hour. Drain well and cool. These sausage rolls freeze well.

Home-Grown Spices

A Danish lady of the 19th century who produced a well-loved cookbook advised her readers to use three "homegrown spices" to prepare food: (1) punctuality (2) a snow-white cloth on a well-laid table and (3) the housewife's gentle friendly face.

Spiced Meat Roll
Rullepølse

Mrs. Evelyn Hansen Behrens, Danish Sisterhood Lodge #60, Albert Lea, Minnesota

- 1 flank beef or lamb
- 3 or 4 thin slices of pork
- 2 tablespoons salt
- 1/2 tablespoon saltpeter
- 1 teaspoon pepper
- 1 chopped onion
- 1/2 teaspoon allspice

Brine:
- 2-1/2 quarts boiling water
- 2 cups salt
- 1/2 teaspoon saltpeter

Remove sinew from meat and cut it so it forms a square or rectangle. Flatten out and sprinkle with seasonings. Lay pork slices on flank. Roll meat tightly so when it is cut it will slice across the grain of meat. Sew ends and sides. Put in cold brine for 10 days.

After 10 days, remove meat from brine, wind securely with cord and put into boiling water. Cook slowly for 2 hours or until tender. Remove from water and press between two flat surfaces until cold. Serve thin slices on bread.

Liver Paste
Dagmar's Leverpostej

Dagmar Jensen, Danish Sisterhood Lodge #7, Clinton, Iowa. Dagmar is an excellent cook whose recipes frequently appear in the Danish Sisterhood News. *This is a traditional recipe.*

 1 pound pork liver
3/4 pound pork fat
 2 tablespoons butter
 2 tablespoons flour
 2 cups milk
 2 eggs
 1 chopped onion
3/4 teaspoon pepper
 1 tablespoon salt
1/2 teaspoon allspice

Put liver and fat through meat grinder about 5 times. In medium skillet, melt butter. Add flour, stirring to blend. Add milk and cook until smooth. Add this cream sauce to liver mixture. Add eggs, chopped onion, and spices. Beat well. Bake in a loaf pan set in a pan of shallow water for 1-1/4 hours at 350°. Cool. Serve as a sandwich spread decorated with pickles.

Danish Liver Loaf
Carmen's Leverpostej

Mrs. Carmen Madson Opdahl, Albert Lea, Minnesota

 2 pounds liver
 1 pound boneless pork
 1 medium onion
 2 beaten eggs
 3 tablespoons flour
 1 cup milk
1/2 teaspoon salt
1/4 teaspoon pepper
   sautéed mushrooms
   cooked, crumbled bacon

Grind liver, pork, and onion. Add eggs, flour, milk, and seasonings. Bake in a well-greased bread pan for about 45 minutes. Pierce with fork, which will come out clean when loaf is done. Garnish with sautéed mushrooms and crisp bacon.

Hot Mustard Sauce
Sennepsovs

Thora Mae Andersen of Solvang, CA

 1 tablespoon superfine dry
   mustard
 1 tablespoon flour
 1 tablespoon sugar
 1 tablespoon vinegar

Mix dry ingredients well. Add vinegar and enough water to make a sauce. It is easy to increase or decrease recipe since you always use equal amounts of each ingredient. Excellent served with ham.

Cheese Bags
Ostebrød

Birte Lund, Funen, Denmark

1-1/2 cups lukewarm water
1 tablespoon yeast
1 cup yogurt
2 tablespoons oil
1 egg
1 teaspoon salt
2 cups whole wheat flour
2 cups rye flour
4 cups unbleached wheat
   flour
Filling:
   4 peeled tomatoes
   3 tablespoons chopped onions
   4 ounces grated cheese
   1 teaspoon oregano
   egg for brushing

Dissolve yeast in lukewarm water. Add remaining ingredients. Knead dough thoroughly and let rise in a warm place for about 45 minutes, while the filling is made.

Filling: Cut tomatoes in wedges and boil with onion until smooth and thick. Stir in cheese and oregano. Cool in refrigerator.

Punch down dough and roll out thinly. Cut in 2-1/2-inch squares. Place 1 teaspoon filling along one side of each square.

Brush with beaten egg around the edge of each square and fold in half. Press edges with a fork. Let rise on a baking sheet for about 15 minutes. Brush surface with egg and bake at 375° for 15 to 20 minutes.

Variation: Squares can be as large as 4"x4". Put filling on and fold in a triangle.

Mushroom Delight
Lækkerchampignon

Else Lassiter of Solvang, California

1-1/2 pounds sliced fresh
   mushrooms
1/4 cup butter
1/2 cup flour
   half-and-half (enough to
    thicken gravy)
   salt and pepper to taste
1/4 cup lemon juice
   patty shells* or white toast
   rounds
   tomato and parsley for garnish

Sauté sliced mushrooms in hot butter. Stir in flour. Add half-and-half, stirring to make a thick gravy. Add salt, pepper, and lemon juice to taste. Serve on lettuce in patty shells or on rounds of white toast. Garnish with tomato slices and parsley. Serve hot as a first course. *Editor's note: A patty shell is an edible baked puff pastry shell that can be filled with fruit or creamed seafood.

Sherry Herring
Sherrysild

From Marianne Larsen, who was born in Vejle, Denmark, and came to the United States in 1967. She and her husband, Uffe, were owners of the Møllekroen Restaurant in Solvang, California, from 1973–2001.

4 Matjes herring
1 chopped onion
1 bunch dill weed
1/4 cup sherry
1/2 cup tomato juice
1 to 2 tablespoons sugar
1/2 teaspoon allspice

Cut herring in 1- to 2-inch pieces. Combine with onion and dill weed. Combine sherry, tomato juice, sugar, and allspice. Pour over first mixture.

Curry Herring
Karrysild

Marianne Larsen of Solvang, CA

4 marinated whole herring
2 hard-cooked eggs
1 chopped onion
1 cup mayonnaise
2 tablespoons cream
2 teaspoons curry powder
  lemon juice
  salt and pepper
  hard-boiled eggs and parsley
  for garnish

Cut herring in small pieces. Slice eggs. Layer herring and eggs in bowl. Put onion on top. Mix mayonnaise with cream and curry powder. Add lemon juice, salt, and pepper to taste. Pour dressing over herring and decorate with sliced hard-cooked eggs and chopped parsley. This can be artfully arranged in a clear glass bowl to show the layers.

Mustard Herring
Sennepsild

This recipe comes from Else Lassiter, who was born in Sønderborg, Denmark, and raised in Haderslev. She came to the United States in 1964, settling in Solvang in 1967.

3 marinated herring or red
  herring
2 tablespoons dry mustard
2 tablespoons sugar
  dash salt and white pepper
1 tablespoon vinegar
1 pint whipping cream,
  whipped
  dill weed

Cut up herring. Arrange on platter. Mix spices, seasonings, and vinegar. Fold in whipped cream. Place a spoonful on each piece of herring. Sprinkle with dill.

Danbo Dip

4 ounces grated Danbo cheese
2 ounces Danish cream cheese
3 tablespoons catsup
5 tablespoons water
2 tablespoons chopped red
  pepper
1 tablespoon chopped green
  pepper
1/4 teaspoon Worcestershire
  sauce

Blend the Danbo and cream cheese. Stir in the catsup, water, chopped peppers, and Worcestershire sauce.

Canapés

Day-old bread is preferred for canapés, as it does not crumble easily when buttered. Shapes may be round, square, or oval. Butter all bread slices before cutting into shapes. Time can be saved by cleaning vegetables and putting the various spreads and ingredients in bowls before the buttering process.

Smoked salmon: Cut salmon slices in halves lengthwise. Fold the salmon like a cornet and press it into the butter with a sprig of dill in the cornet.

Shrimp: Put a dab of mayonnaise in the middle of the canapé and shrimp on top. Insert toothpick into a bit of lettuce and pin it to the canapé.

Caviar: Spread caviar on bread like butter. Fasten a lemon wedge to the canapé with a toothpick.

Salami: Press small slices of salami on buttered bread. Larger slices may be rolled or folded together like a cornet and pressed into the butter. Sprinkle with chopped chives.

Ham: Place a thin slice of folded ham on bread. Insert toothpick into small tomato wedge or carrot slice, then through ham and bread. Garnish with parsley sprig.

Tongue: Roll thin slices of tongue and place on bread. Insert toothpick in small square of cream cheese, then into bread. Garnish with watercress.

Liver Pâté: Soften pâté with cream and mound on bread. Snip cucumber slice in half and overlap cut edges to make a cone. Insert toothpick through cucumber into bread.

Danish blue cheese: Cut cheese into small cubes using a thin heated knife.

Danbo cheese: Top small cube of cheese with radish slice held in place by a toothpick.

Samsoe: Insert toothpick into stuffed olive, then into a cube of Samsoe cheese.

Bacon rolls: Roll half a slice of bacon around a cocktail sausage and secure with toothpick. Fry in a little butter until golden and crispy.

Blue cheese nuts: Cut blue cheese into small cubes with small heated knife. Place a cube of cheese between two English walnut halves and press together.

Danish blue with grapes: Secure a thick round slice of cheese and a dark grape with a toothpick.

Havarti cubes: Combine Havarti cheese with parsley sprigs between two radish slices or tomato wedges with a sprig of parsley on top.

Tybo or Samsoe cubes: Combine cheese with mandarin orange segments, pineapple chunks, and cocktail cherries or grapes.

Open-faced Sandwiches

Smørrebrød is a Danish luncheon staple and the mainstay of easy, elegant entertaining. Eye appeal is as important as taste, and because these lovely little sandwiches are eaten with a knife and fork, the sky's the limit when it comes to ingredients!

Ingredients:

thin slices of	caviar	
hearty bread	shrimp	
cut in half	cheeses	
butter	oysters	
Boston lettuce	anchovies	
herring	crab	
salami	scrambled eggs	
roast beef	sardines	
liver pâté	pressed lamb	

Garnish:

radish slices	dill
parsley	chives
watercress	olives
tomato slices	
fresh fruit	
sliced hard-	
boiled eggs	
onion rings	
cucumbers	

Be sure bread is sliced thin and cut in half. Cover the entire slice with butter to keep moist toppings from soaking through. Cover one corner with a leaf of lettuce. Use plenty of topping so that no bread shows. Folding meat slices and overlapping cheese makes more room.

The only limit to the possibilities of *smørrebrød* is the time and imagination of the creator.

Possible combinations:

White bread and lox, mayonnaise, and sweet pickles; chopped chicken, pineapple, and mayonnaise; chopped shrimp, cucumber slices, French dressing, and radishes; lobster and asparagus mixed with mayonnaise.

Rye bread and thinly sliced roast beef, cream cheese, and raw onion rings; liver pâté, sautéed mushrooms, strips of bacon, and lettuce; Danish blue cheese, onion rings, and sieved hard-boiled eggs; sliced corned beef, watercress, and sliced hard-boiled eggs; chopped and cooked chicken liver, crumbled bacon, sliced tomatoes, and lemon juice; sliced pork roast, prunes, and sliced oranges; sliced boiled new potatoes, bacon strips, cocktail sausages, tomato slivers, and chopped parsley.

Either bread and sliced *frikadeller*, pickled beets and cucumber slices; pickled herring and sliced sweet onion; salami, sliced jellied consommé, and a dab of mustard; blue cheese mixed with Cherry Heering liqueur.

Cheese Tray

Which Danish cheese is which? *Samsoe* has a mild, nutlike flavor. *Danbo* is mild and firm and comes also with caraway seed. *Esrom* has a slightly aromatic flavor; *Svenbo* is mild, *Emmentaler* is nutlike in flavor, and *Saint Paulin* is "piquant," as is *Danish Feta.* Danish *Camembert* has a mushroom-like flavor, and Danish *Brie* is mild and aromatic. *Tybo* and *Elbo* are mild, and only the Danish blue cheese, *Danablu*, is characterized as "sharp and distinctive."

The Danish Cheese Export Board recommends the following quantities on a cheese tray for **six** people:

1 pound 2 ounces Samsoe
1 pound 2 ounces Havarti
9 ounces Danablu
7 ounces Danish Camembert

A cheese buffet for **twelve** calls for:

11 ounces Danbo
12 ounces Tybo with caraway seed
1 pound Havarti 60%
13 ounces Danablu
1 pound 6 ounces Danish Brie
11 ounces Camembert

Both tray and buffet are rounded out with grapes, red and green peppers, radishes, cucumber slices, and walnuts.

Easy Does It Not

The tender loving care lavished on Danish cookery is repaid by elegant taste, texture and appearance. Without a trace of impatience, a true Danish cook will grind meat five times, simmer a vegetable for three hours, or soak meat in brine for days. She'll chop and stir and hover, committed as fervently as any artist to an end result that will delight the eye and the palate.

However, not all Danish recipes are complicated and time-consuming. With some, it's a matter of collecting first-rate ingredients and combining them beautifully.

If you really want to cook in the Danish mode, you must plunge in without counting the costs. Top grade ingredients are essential. If a recipe calls for butter, then butter it should be—for the sake of flavor. Unless you're willing to settle for less, whipping cream should come from the dairy. And so it goes.

Danish cookery is about as far from fast foods and instant everything as you can get, but the rewards are great. How sweet it is to hear, *"Tak for mad!"* ("Thanks for the food!") and answer, *"Velbekomme!"* ("May it become you well!")

The Rock Was Warm

According to an old tale, St. Peter puts a warm rock into the ground at the end of February to start the spring thaw.

The Raised Glass

The favorite drink of the Danes is aquavit, which means "water of life." The clear liquor is made from potatoes or grain, and this vodka of the north can be flavored with many herbs, including dill and caraway. It must be cold with ice on the bottle and dew on the glass, and it's often consumed with a sidecar of good Danish beer. To drink it in the Danish manner, raise your glass, nod slightly and say, *"Skaal,"* drink the contents and say, "Ah!" as you set the glass down.

Another distinctly Danish delight is Peter Heering liqueur, a cherry-flavored liquid velvet that looks as lovely as it tastes. Those who prefer their liquid refreshment without a kick can say *"Skaal!"* with punch that's both pretty and delicious. Each letter in the word *"Skaal"* has a meaning: S is for togetherness, K is for love, A is for many talents, the second A is for longevity, and the final L is for luck.

High-Spirited Drinks

From the Danish Information Office

King Peter

1 part Cherry Heering
2 parts tonic water
  lemon juice to taste
  ice cubes

Trivoli By Night

1 part Cherry Heering
1 part pineapple juice
1 part Kahlúa liqueur
  ice cubes
  garnish with cherries and
    lemon slice

Black Dane

1 part Kahlúa liqueur
1 part Jubilaeum aquavit
  ice cubes

Danish Mary

1 part Aalborg Taffel aquavit
1 part tomato juice
  dash of Tabasco™
  celery stalk

Ruby Red Frost Punch

From Esther Andersen, Dike, Iowa

2 cups cranberry juice
1 cup sugar
1 pint raspberry sherbet
1-1/2 cups fresh lemon juice
2 (28-ounce) bottles chilled ginger
  ale

Apple Shrub

Put a small ball of **lime sherbet** in a juice glass, fill with **apple cider** and serve.

Salads

When eating is one of life's greatest pleasures, the salad is much more than the austere staple of a grim diet. It's piquant, pretty, savory, and often sensational. Creating a salad to please both the eye and the palate with ingredients as fresh as a newly opened flower delights the Danes.

Salmon Salad Mold
Lakssalat

Esther Andersen, Dike, Iowa

2 packages lemon-flavored
   gelatin
2 cups boiling water
1/2 cup mayonnaise
1/2 cup coffee cream
1/2 cup pimiento cheese
1/2 teaspoon onion salt
1/2 cup cooked peas
1 (1-pound) flaked red salmon,
   1 cup diced celery
1/2 chopped green pepper
   1 stuffed olive
   3 sliced hard-boiled eggs

Dissolve gelatin in water. Add remaining ingredients, except eggs and olive; mix well. Use egg slices in bottom of fish-shaped mold for "backbone." Pour mixture into mold and chill. Unmold onto a bed of leaf lettuce. Use stuffed olive slices for eyes.

Crab Salad
Krabbesalat

Birte Lund, Funen, Denmark

1 cup mayonnaise
   tarragon vinegar to taste
   salt to taste
   paprika to taste
1 tablespoon tomato purée
1/2 pound crabmeat
1 stalk celery, diced
4 large tomatoes
   alfalfa sprouts

Mix mayonnaise with vinegar, salt, and paprika to taste. Add tomato purée, then crabmeat and celery. Neatly slice tops off tomatoes and scoop out seeds, fill with salad and sprinkle with alfalfa sprouts on top. Serves 4. Good with hot French bread.

Still Soft?

Danish cooks of the long ago are said to have timed the perfect soft-boiled egg by saying the Lord's Prayer backwards twice. Sounds unlikely.

Shrimp Salad
Rejesalat

Else Lassiter, Solvang, California

1/2 cup mayonnaise
1/2 cup sour cream
1 to 2 tablespoons cocktail sauce
3 to 4 tablespoons sherry
    dash white pepper
1 pound cooked shrimp
1/2 pound fresh sliced mushrooms
    or 1 small can sliced mush-
    rooms
1 (8-ounce) can cut asparagus
1 can pineapple slices, drained
    lemon for garnish

Stir together the first five ingredients. Fold in cooked shrimp, sliced mushrooms, and asparagus. Serve on slices of pineapple on leaf lettuce. Garnish with lemon slices.

Sweet Pea Salad
Ærtesalat

Nathalie Andersen, Solvang, California

1 (1-pound) can sweet peas,
    drained
4 or 5 sliced sweet gherkin pickles
3 or 4 stalks celery, cut in small
    pieces
1/2 cup salad dressing
3 or 4 tablespoons pickle juice

Combine peas, pickles, and celery. Mix salad dressing and pickle juice. Pour over first mixture and mix lightly.

Danish Chicken Salad
Kyllingsalat

Danish Agricultural Producers

6 ounces cream cheese
2 tablespoons milk
1 pound cooked chicken
    (diced or sliced)
2 tablespoons butter
2 ounces split blanched almonds
1 (10-1/2-ounce) can asparagus
    salt and pepper

Mash cream cheese with milk until soft and well blended, then stir in pieces of chicken, reserving a few pieces for decoration. Melt butter in frying pan and fry almonds until golden. Drain asparagus and cut 2/3 of it into 1-inch pieces. Stir these with almonds into chicken and cream cheese mixture. Season with salt and pepper. Garnish with remaining chicken and asparagus.

Tivoli Salad
Tivoli Salat

A festive salad from the Danish Cheese Export Board

1 cup diced Havarti cheese
4 medium tomatoes, quartered
  and drained
1 cup finely chopped cucumber
1/2 cup chopped green pepper
1 cup diced cooked ham
Dressing:
1/4 cup mayonnaise
1/2 cup dairy sour cream
1/2 teaspoon Dijon style mustard
1/2 teaspoon curry powder
1/2 teaspoon grated onion
1 tablespoon fresh lemon
  juice
salt and cayenne to taste

In a large bowl, combine cheese, vegetables, and meat. Blend dressing ingredients, pour over salad and toss gently. Chill. Serve with warm French bread.

Carrot Salad
Gulerodsalat

Frieda Hansen, Clinton, Iowa

1 (11-ounce) can tomato soup
1 cup sugar
1/4 cup Wesson oil
1/4 cup vinegar
1 teaspoon dry mustard
1 teaspoon Worcestershire
  sauce
1/2 teaspoon salt
2 pounds carrots, peeled and
  sliced
1 diced medium onion
1 chopped green pepper
1/2 cup chopped celery

Combine soup, sugar, oil, vinegar, mustard, Worcestershire®, and salt. Cook for 5 minutes and cool. Cook carrots until tender, drain and add onion, green pepper, and celery. Pour sauce over vegetables and marinate overnight.

Variation: Hanne Nelson of Racine, Wisconsin, uses 1 teaspoon coarse pepper in her recipe. The recipe, called carrot relish in Racine, makes approximately 2 quarts.

Olive Scotland Ferguson of Walnut, Iowa, says, "The drained dressing makes an excellent salad dressing when the carrots are gone. It is tasty to serve on lettuce salad to accompany meat or casseroles or to serve as a separate relish."

Copenhagen Salad
København Salat

Danish Agricultural Producers

6 ounces Danablu (blue cheese)
1/2 pound black grapes
4 ounces shelled walnuts
1 (11-ounce) can mandarin
   oranges (drained)
white wine or liqueur

Cut cheese into 3/4-inch cubes (easy if cheese is well chilled.) Mix with halved and seeded grapes, halved walnuts, and mandarin oranges. Just before serving, sprinkle with a little white wine or some liqueur.

Lettuce Salad with Cream
Salat med Fløde

Julie Jensen-McDonald, Davenport, Iowa, says, "Fresh garden lettuce in this tangy cream is one of my happiest early taste memories."

1 head iceberg or red leaf lettuce
1-1/2 cups cream
1-1/2 teaspoons sugar
1 tablespoon vinegar

Wash the lettuce, drain, and tear into small pieces. In a blender, whip the cream slightly with sugar and vinegar. (If only sour cream is used, omit vinegar and use only 1 teaspoon of sugar). Pour over lettuce and toss lightly.

Cucumber Salad
Agurkesalat

Myrna Oleson of Racine, Wisconsin, first enjoyed cucumbers prepared this way when she visited her husband's Danish aunt. A young man from Denmark who stayed with the Olesons also fixed cucumbers this way.

2 cups peeled, thinly sliced
   cucumbers
2 tablespoons salt
1/2 cup white vinegar
1/2 cup sugar

Soak the cucumbers in salt with enough water to cover for one hour. Squeeze out the salt water. Heat the vinegar and dissolve the sugar in it. (Some cooks add a couple tablespoons of water to dilute the vinegar.) Add the cucumbers and chill for one hour to preserve crispness before serving.

Variation: Add thinly sliced onion rings. This same mixture of sugar and vinegar can be used with thinly sliced cooked beets.

Curry Salad
Karrysalat

Julie Jensen-McDonald, Davenport, Iowa

- 1 cup mayonaise
- 4 ounces dairy sour cream
- 2–3 teaspoons curry powder
- 1–2 teaspoons lemon juice
- 1 (8-ounce) container pickled herring fillets
- 6 hard-boiled eggs
- 1 small chopped onion
- lettuce leaves
- watercress

Blend mayonaise and sour cream. Season to taste with curry powder and lemon juice. Cut herring into diagonal slices, reserving 3 or 4 slices for garnish. Reserve 1 egg for garnish and quarter the rest. Fold herring, eggs, and chopped onion into mayonaise mixture. Turn into salad bowl and garnish with reserved sliced egg, and herring slices, lettuce leaves, and watercress.

He who would make
 a fool of himself
  finds many to help him.
   —Danish proverb

He who gives to me
 teaches me to give.
  —Danish proverb

Too little or too much
 spoils anything.
  —Danish proverb

Beet and Onion Salad
Rødbede og Iøgsalat

Olive Scotland Ferguson, Walnut, Iowa

- 1 medium onion, sliced thinly into rings
- 2 No. 2 cans beets, drained

Dressing:
- 1/4 cup salad oil
- 1/4 cup sugar
- 2 tablespoons vinegar
- 1 teaspoon lemon juice
- 1/4 teaspoon salt
- 1/8 teaspoon dry mustard
- 1/8 teaspoon paprika
- 1/8 teaspoon celery seed, optional
- pinch of garlic salt
- dash of pepper

Mix dressing, pour over beets and onion rings. Refrigerate, covered, overnight. Serves 10–12.

Vegetables

Denmark is a farming nation, and whatever the Danes can grow, they can cook with style. Matchmakers at heart, they often marry their magnificent farm and dairy products to the yield of their gardens with the happiest results. Potatoes are the mainstay of many a meal, and the Danes see to it that they're never dull. The vegetable conspicuously missing from the national cuisine seems to be the green bean. The Danes concentrate on vegetables that can be grown through the winter.

Hot Potato Salad
Kartoffelsalat

Julie Jensen-McDonald

4 slices bacon
1 large onion, quartered
1 teaspoon sugar
1/2 teaspoon salt
2 tablespoons butter
3 tablespoons vinegar
6 to 8 cold boiled medium-sized
    potatoes
2 tablespoons cream
dash pepper

Fry bacon, drain and set aside. Peel onion, quarter and boil in small amount of water. Add sugar, salt, butter, and vinegar. Cook until onions are transparent. Slice potatoes and add slowly to the onion mixture, turning carefully to avoid breaking the potatoes. Add cream, pepper, and crumbled bacon. Serve hot.

> The pot boils best
>
> on one's own hearth.
>
> —Danish proverb

Hasselbach Potatoes
Hasselbach Kartofler

Birte Lund, Funen, Denmark, says this is a pretty way to serve the sometimes pedestrian potato.

medium sized potatoes
cooking oil
butter or margarine
salt
dry bread crumbs

Peel potatoes and make thick slices, cutting just far enough to leave the slices connected at the base. (Place potatoes in the bowl of a wooden spoon while cutting to avoid slicing through the base.) Roll in cooking oil, cover tops with butter and salt and bake about 45 minutes at 350°. Before placing in the broiler for the last 10 minutes, baste with melted butter and sprinkle with dry bread crumbs.

Copenhagen Potatoes
Kobenhavn Kartofler

From Danish Agricultural Producers

1-1/2 pounds potatoes
1/2 pound bacon
2 tablespoons butter
3 tablespoons vinegar
1 tablespoon chopped parsley
salt and pepper to taste

Cook unpeeled potatoes in boiling water. Drain, remove skins, and cut into cubes. Cut bacon into squares and fry crisp in butter. Add potatoes, vinegar, and parsley. Season with salt and pepper and toss lightly until well mixed and hot. Serves four.

Carameled Potatoes
Brunede Kartofler

Julie Jensen McDonald

2 tablespoons granulated sugar
1/4 cup butter
1-1/2 pounds plain boiled potatoes

Put sugar into a heavy frying pan or saucepan over low heat. Stir gently until sugar melts and turns golden. Add butter and allow to melt. Stir in drained potatoes and heat gently until well glazed. Makes four servings.

Flour and Paprika

To fry cooked potatoes to a perfect brown, sprinkle them with flour and paprika.

Red Cabbage
Rødkål

*Mrs. Evelyn Hansen Behrens,
Albert Lea, Minnesota*

1/4 cup butter
5 pounds red cabbage, finely cut
1/2 cup vinegar
1/2 cup sugar
1 tablespoon salt

Brown butter lightly in a kettle. Add finely cut cabbage and stir well. Add vinegar, sugar, and salt. Let simmer 2 to 3 hours. To reduce cabbage odor, bring the mixture to a boil, then place in a 325° oven in a covered container for two hours. The flavor is even better when reheated.

Variation: Stir in 1/4 cup currant jelly 10 minutes before cooking is done.

Creamed Mushrooms
Champignons i Ostesovs

Birte Lund, Denmark

2 cups sliced mushrooms
1 tablespoon butter
1/2 tablespoon cornstarch
1 cup half and half
1 cup shredded mild cheese
dash of salt
dash of cayenne pepper
1 tablespoon dry sherry
4 slices buttered toast
lettuce for garnish

Sauté mushrooms in butter until golden brown. Mix cornstarch with half and half. Add to mushrooms and simmer, stirring until thickened. Fold in cheese until it melts smoothly into the sauce. Add salt, cayenne pepper, and sherry. Serve over toast. Serves four.

Creamed Kale
Grønlangkål

Betty Hansen Møllerskov, Racine, Wisconsin

> 2 stalks kale
> 3 tablespoons butter
> 3 tablespoons flour
> 2 cups milk
> 1 teaspoon salt
> 1 tablespoon sugar

Clean kale thoroughly in cold water. Remove stalks and center veins of the leaves. Cook until barely tender in salted water. Drain well. Chop finely. Melt butter; gradually stir in flour. Mix well, gradually adding milk. Cook until thick and smooth. Stir in chopped kale. Add salt and sugar and heat thoroughly.

This Danish vegetable is usually served with *medisterpølse* (pork sausage) and *brunede kartofler* (small round browned potatoes).

Spinach Soufflé
Spinatsouffles

Esther Anderson, Dike, Iowa

> 2 cups cooked spinach
> 1/2 teaspoon salt
>   pepper to taste
> 1/4 cup melted butter
> 3 eggs, separated
> 1 cup cream or milk
> 1 teaspoon baking powder

Chop spinach; add salt, pepper, butter, beaten egg yolks, and cream. Beat whites until frothy, add baking powder and beat stiff. Fold into mixture. Bake in buttered casserole 50 minutes at 350°.

Variation: Broccoli may be substituted for spinach. If so, add 1 tablespoon lemon juice, some sharp cheese, and minced garlic.

The
road to a
friend's
house is
never long.
—Danish proverb

From the French

The Danish cuisine has borrowed much from the French, employing that subtlety and sophistication in a unique way.

Main Dishes

Danish entrées never hide behind sauces. They wear them like handsome accessories. Danes have pioneered sophisticated agricultural techniques to produce food of the highest quality, and nothing less will do. They boast that "no one ever dies of starvation in Denmark," a wry and typical understatement in a land where excellence and elegance are twin attributes of the daily fare.

Roast Goose
Stegt Gås

From the Danish Sisterhood News. Goose is the traditional heart of the Christmas feast—much more moist than Turkey.

**1 (10-pound) goose
salt and pepper
1-1/2 cups peeled, cored, and
sliced apples
1 cup soaked, pitted prunes
4 cups boiling water**

Season the goose inside and out with salt and pepper and stuff with apples and prunes. Put in a large pan and brown goose on all sides in hot oven. Add 4 cups boiling water and baste. Roast for 3 hours at 325°. For crisp skin, pour 2 tablespoons water over the goose and let brown 15 minutes. Skim fat from drippings, strain, and thicken for gravy.

Serve with red cabbage, carmeled potatoes, white potatoes, and green salad.

Apple Stuffing For Goose
Æblefars til Gås

Julie Jensen-McDonald

Julie Jensen McDonald offers this roast goose stuffing alternative in her Definitely Danish *(1993).*

**1 quart of bread crumbs,
rather dry and not too fine
1/2 cup butter or margarine
1 quart coarsely chopped
apples
1 cup chopped celery
1 medium-sized chopped
onion
1-1/2 teaspoons salt
1/2 teaspoon celery salt
1/4 teaspoon pepper
1/8 teaspoon cloves
1/4 teaspoon cinnamon
1 cup of hot water**

Moisten the above ingredients with the 1 cup of hot water and stuff your goose.

Three women and a goose make a market.

—Danish proverb

130—

Roast Duck
Stegt And

Mrs. Betty (Hansen) Møllerskov, Racine, Wisconsin

1 (5 to 7-pound) duck
salt
3 tart apples
1/2 pound prunes

Wash, clean, and dry duck. Rub inside with salt. Stuff with apples, which have been pared, cored, and quartered, and with prunes, which have been soaked and pitted. Sprinkle duck all over with salt and place in an ungreased roasting pan, breast side up. Roast uncovered in 325° oven, 45 minutes per pound. Do not prick skin with fork. Remove excess fat from pan during roasting.

Copenhagen Schnitzel
Københavner Schnitzel

Birte Lund from Funen, Denmark

1/2 cup whipping cream
10 almonds
2 teaspoons lemon juice
2 apples, peeled and sliced in thick slices
1-1/2 pounds veal fillet
1/4 cup butter
salt and pepper
12 green grapes

Whip the cream. Cut the almonds in pieces and mix in the whipped cream with the lemon juice. Peel the apples and cut into thick rings. Cut the fillet into 4 slices and brown for one minute on each side in an ungreased pan. Turn heat down and brown in the butter 3 minutes on each side. Season with salt and pepper and remove meat to a warm place while cooking the apple rings in the pan.

Lay an apple ring on each fillet, fill center with whipped cream mixture, and decorate with green grapes.

This handsome entrée may be served with hasselbach potatoes and a green salad.

Where there is discipline
there is virtue
Where there is peace
There is plenty.
—Danish proverb

Danish Veal "Birds"
Benløse Fugle

Esther Andersen, Dike, Iowa, says, "In some parts of Denmark, a strip of bacon is wrapped around each piece of veal or steak."

1-1/2 pounds veal or round steak, 1/2-inch thick
1/4 cup chopped onion
3 tablespoons butter
2 cups soft bread crumbs
1 tablespoon parsley flakes
1/2 cup chopped celery
1/2 teaspoon salt
1 tablespoon water
flour to coat
1 (10-1/2-ounce) can cream of mushroom soup

Pound meat well. Sauté onion lightly in butter; add bread crumbs, parsley, celery, salt, and water to make a dressing. Cut meat in four pieces, placing dressing on each piece. Roll up and fasten with toothpicks. Season and roll in flour. Brown well. Add a little water and the undiluted soup. Cover and simmer until tender, about 1-1/2 hours, adding water if needed during cooking.

Danish Cordon Bleu

From Denmark Cheese Association, Aarhus, Denmark

4 lean sirloin steaks (1/3 pound each)
1 teaspoon Dijon mustard
4 thin slices Danish ham
4 thin slices *Svenbo* or *Danbo* cheese (mild, light yellow cheese)
1/3 cup flour
1 teaspoon salt
1/2 teaspoon pepper
1 egg, slightly beaten
2/3 cup bread crumbs
1/3 cup butter
lemon and parsley for garnish

Pound steaks until approximately 4 x 7-inches. Spread with mustard. Top each with slice of ham and cheese (both slices smaller than steaks). Fold steaks over, secure with skewers. Mix flour with seasonings. Dip each steak in flour on both sides, then in egg, finally in bread crumbs. Fry in butter for 4 minutes on each side until golden brown. Garnish. Serve with vegetables. Makes 4 servings.

Things never go so well
that one should have no fear
nor so ill
that one should have
no hope.
—Danish proverb

Meat Balls
Frikadeller

From a Christmas smorgasbord menu at Dana College, Blair, NE. Frikadeller *recipes were also submitted by Carmen Madson Opdahl and Evelyn Hansen Behrens of Albert Lea, Minnesota.*

1 pound ground beef (round steak or chuck)
1/2 pound lean pork
1/4 cup flour
1 teaspoon salt
1/2 teaspoon pepper
1 small grated onion
2 eggs
1 cup milk
4 tablespoons margarine

Mix the first six ingredients thoroughly. Add eggs, milk, and margarine. Form into 8 patties, and fry in butter at 300° (electric skillet) until brown. Turn down heat to 250° and cover for 30 minutes to thoroughly cook.

God gives every bird its food
but does not
drop it into the nest.
—Danish proverb

Roast Pork with Apples and Prunes
Flæskesteg med Æbler og Svedsker

Julie Jensen-McDonald

4 pounds loin of pork (with rind, if possible)
salt and pepper
3 to 4 apples
1/2 pound prunes, cooked

With a sharp knife, score pork rind with close cuts and place it rind-side down in a roasting pan. Add enough water to cover bottom of pan. Bake at 400° for about 25 minutes. Turn meat, sprinkle with salt and pepper, and return to oven. Lower the heat to 350° and roast until the meat is tender and the rind is crisp (about 1-1/2 hours more).

Peel and quarter the apples and poach in lightly sweetened water. Serve with roast and prunes. Serve with red cabbage.

Variations: Prunes may be marinated in port wine several hours before cooking or baking. Apple halves may be poached in 1 quart water and 1 cup of sugar for about 10 minutes. Core the apples carefully to make a nest for the prunes.

Pork Tenderloin with Olive Stuffing
Svinemørbrad med Olivenfyld

Recipe from Karin Jensen, Denmark

2 extra lean pork tenderloins
butter for browning
1-1/2 cups dry white wine
1/2 cup whipping cream

Stuffing:
  2 slices white bread, crusts
    removed, cubed
  5 ounces stuffed olives,
    chopped
  1/2 bunch parsley, chopped
  4 cloves garlic
    salt, pepper, and basil to
    taste

Insert handle of wooden spoon lengthwise through center of raw meat. Combine stuffing ingredients and let sit for 15 minutes before filling the tenderloins. Place stuffing in hole in meat, pushing to fill. Melt butter in a heavy skillet to brown the filled tenderloins thoroughly on all sides. Combine wine and whipping cream to pour over the meat and cook in this liquid for 15 minutes on each side. Serve with hasselbach potatoes and tossed salad.

Pork Sausage
Medisterpølse

Nathalie Andersen, Solvang, CA

5 pounds lean pork shoulder,
  ground 3 times
1 large onion, grated
1 tablespoon salt
1 teaspoon pepper
1/2 teaspoon allspice
1/2 teaspoon cloves
1 cup stock (chicken broth)

Add the seasonings to the meat, mix well. Add the stock. Press into casings (bought at the butcher's) and tie at regular intervals to make links. Fry in a skillet or bake in the oven.

Cabbage Rolls
Hvidkålsrouletter

This recipe comes from Thora Mae Andersen, mother of one of Solvang's Danish Maids.

1 pound ground beef
1/2 pound ground pork
1 small onion, grated
1 egg
1/2 cup milk
  salt and pepper to taste
1 large head cabbage

Mix together all ingredients except cabbage. Holding cabbage under hot water, pull off leaves. Using two or three leaves for each roll, put a large scoop of meat mixture inside. Wrap and tie with string. Boil rolls in water 30 to 40 minutes. Remove rolls, untie string and serve. Makes approximately six or seven rolls. Serve with boiled and buttered potatoes. An excellent boiled dinner!

Boiled Cod
Kogt Torsk

Penny Davidsen of Iowa City, Iowa, writes, "My husband Oluf's mother taught me how to boil cod. I met Oluf in Italy. He was from Denmark and working with Danish Quakers and I for the American Friends rebuilding a hospital that had been bombed in World War II."

1-1/2 pounds cod
1-1/2 quarts water
1-1/2 teaspoons salt

Boil cod until it flakes. Save the water to use for the sauce made with dark mustard.

Mustard Gravy for Cod Fish
Sennepsovs Kogt Torsk

Inga Nielsen Harmansen of Racine, Wisconsin, came to America from Denmark in 1955. This recipe was her mother's.

3 tablespoons melted magarine
3 tablespoons flour
1 cup fish water from boiling cod
1 cup milk
1 tablespoon dark Danish fish or Dijon mustard
1/2 teaspoon salt

Add flour to melted margarine. Stir thoroughly and gradually add milk and fish water. Cook until thickened. Stir in mustard and salt. Serves four.

Shrimp Au Gratin
Rejes au Gratin

Denmark Cheese Association, Aarhus, Denmark

6 slices French bread
1/2 cup mayonnaise
1/2 cup dairy sour cream
2 teaspoons fresh lemon juice
dash salt
dash cayenne pepper
1 pound small shrimp, cooked and cleaned
8 egg whites
2 cups shredded *Danbo* or *Tybo* cheese (mild flavored)

Toast bread lightly on both sides. Mix mayonnaise, sour cream, lemon juice, and spices. Fold in well drained shrimp. Whip egg whites until stiff and fold in cheese. Spoon shrimp mixture onto bread. Top with spoonfuls of cheese mixture to cover shrimp. Bake at 475° for about 10 minutes until golden brown. Serve immediately. Makes 6 servings.

Soups

Danes love comfort—soft cushions to lean on, the absence of drafts, and the inner glow created by an excellent hot soup. However, winter is not the only season when they glory in soup. Dear to the Danish palate are the sweet fruit soups that are delicious heated or chilled, and many Danish soups are inseparable from dumplings.

The Danish Sisterhood News suggests a balanced diet of soups as followed: From the meat group—split pea with ham, bean with beef and vegetable. Bread and cereal group—beef noodle, chicken noodle, and minestrone. Milk and dairy—cream of celery, cream of potato, and chowders. Fruit and vegetable group—chicken vegetable, beef vegetable, tomato, and fruit soups.

Danish Chicken Soup
Hønsekødsuppe

Danish Sisterhood News

1 large soup hen
1 soup wisp*
2 or 3 parsnips, scraped and diced
2 teaspoons salt
Danish dumplings (recipe on page 138)

Cut hen in pieces. Place in cold water to make a good soup or in boiling water if you want chicken dinner. Simmer for 1 to 2 hours. Add the soup wisp, parsnips, and salt. Simmer another hour, skimming occasionally. Remove wisp and serve with dumplings.

*A soup wisp is a tied bundle of parsley, leeks, and celery tops.

Meatballs for Soup
Kødboller

Danish Sisterhood News

1 pound round steak, finely ground
2 eggs, slightly beaten
3 tablespoons flour
salt and pepper

Have meat ground 3 or 4 times. Mix ingredients and make meatballs the size of a large marble. Drop them into boiling salt water. Simmer, turning them, or cook covered. These are done when they puff, and it takes just a few minutes. Keep hot in broth.

Even clever hens
sometimes lay their eggs
among nettles.

—Danish proverb

Lobster Soup
Hummersupper

This recipe is from Birte Lund, a teacher and writer from Funen, Denmark, who lived in Davenport, Iowa, while her husband completed his chiropractic training.

2 whole lobsters
3 large white onions
1 leek or 2 green onions
1 stalk celery
1 carrot
8 cups chicken broth
1/4 cup butter
4 tablespoons flour
2 egg yolks
    salt to taste
4 tablespoons sherry
1 can cut asparagus, drained,
    liquid reserved

Boil live lobsters about 20 minutes in lightly salted water. Discard water. Cut lobster meat into small pieces. Set aside. Combine vegetables (except asparagus) and chicken broth, boiling gently for 1 hour. Strain broth and put vegetables into a bowl. Melt butter; add flour and stir until bubbly. Gradually add broth to the butter and flour, bringing it to a boil with each addition. Beat egg yolks with asparagus liquid and a little of the boiled soup. Combine this mixture with all of the soup, and do not allow to boil further. Add salt and wine, then warmed lobster meat and asparagus. This recipe serves six and is good accompanied by French bread.

Salmon Soup
Laksesuppe

This recipe is from Norma Scherff of Davenport, Iowa, whose mother was born in Copenhagen, Denmark.

1 medium chopped onion
1/2 teaspoon celery salt
1 quart milk
1 (1-pound) can pink salmon,
    drained (skin and bones removed)
salt and pepper to taste
butter (optional)

In a medium skillet, cook onion with celery salt and enough water to cover until tender. Add milk and salmon to onion and water and heat but do not boil. Season to taste and put a dot of butter in each bowl of soup before serving, if desired. Serves four. For the weight conscious, skim milk may be substituted.

Don't sail out
further than
you can row back.
—Danish proverb

Danish Dumplings
Danske Melboller

Miss Marjorie K. Severtsen, Albert Lea, Minnesota

1/4 cup butter
1 cup water
1 cup flour
1/4 teaspoon salt
3 eggs

Combine butter and water and boil. Remove from heat and stir in the flour. Cool slightly. Add salt. Add eggs one at a time, beating briskly each time. Drop by teaspoon into hot, not boiling, broth.

Variation: Recipes for Danish dumplings abound. Carmen Madson Opdahl of Albert Lea, Minnesota, uses milk instead of water and doubles the butter and salt in her Danish dumplings for soup.

Esther's Split Pea Soup
Grønærtsuppe

Esther Andersen, Dike, Iowa

2 cups split peas
6 to 8 cups water
large ham bone
1 onion
3 whole cloves
salt and pepper to taste

Soak peas overnight, then cook with rest of ingredients slowly for 2 to 3 hours.

Kale Soup
Grønkålssuppe

Anna Nielsen of Solvang, CA

ham shank or soup bone
1 medium onion, chopped
3/4 cup oatmeal
10 to 12 curly kale leaves

Make soup stock of ham shank or soup bone. Remove shank or soup bone. Let stock stand overnight and skim off fat. Add onion and oatmeal to stock and heat. Add kale and cook slowly until kale is tender. Cut some of the ham into pieces and add to soup. If necessary, add salt.

Rum Soup
Romsuppe

Julie Jensen McDonald writes, "This soup is great for a cold winter day."

2 egg yolks
1/4 cup sugar
1 tablespoon flour (or 1/4 cup sago—see page 139)
2 quarts milk
1/2 cup rum

Beat egg yolks; beat in sugar and flour. Place in large serving bowl. Scald milk and pour slowly over mixture. Stir in the rum. Serve with zwieback.

If sago is used, boil milk and slowly stir in sago and a pinch of salt. Cook slowly about 20 minutes, until sago is clear, before pouring over the egg, sugar, and flour mixture and adding the rum.

Elderberry Soup
Hyldebærsuppe

Julie Jensen-McDonald says, "My grandmother, Mette Mare Ibsen Faurschou, thought that elderberries were good for anything that ailed us and just plain good. We picked ours in the woods. Elderberries may not be available at the supermarket, but blueberries, black currants, or other fruits may be substituted."

1 pound elderberries
1-1/2 quarts water
2 apples, pared and diced
2 whole cloves
1 stick cinnamon
1/2 cup sugar
1-1/2 tablespoons cornstarch

Cook elderberries in water until tender. Strain and discard pulp. Cook diced apples, cloves, cinnamon, and sugar in the soup until the apples are tender. Add cornstarch mixed with small amount of water and simmer until thickened. Serve hot or cold. Serves four to six.

Sago

Sago is a thickening agent used widely in Scandinavian countries. It must be soaked an hour, and then drained, before using. It is not readily available in U.S. supermarkets, and tapioca may be substituted for it.

Orange Soup
Appelsinsuppe

Julie Jensen-McDonald writes, "We seldom saw an orange in my childhood, and this piquant soup was a great treat."

1/4 cup butter
1/3 cup flour
6 cups boiling water
2 eggs
1/2 cup sugar
1/4 teaspoon salt
    juice of 4 oranges and a bit
    of rind
    juice of 1 lemon

In the soup pot, melt butter and blend in flour. Gradually add boiling water and boil slowly until thickened. Beat eggs with sugar and salt and combine with a little of the cooked mixture. Return the egg mixture to the pot. Cook over very low heat for five minutes, stirring constantly, while adding juice of the oranges and the lemon plus a bit of orange rind. Serve with rusks (a small dried bisket or re-baked bread).

Honor the tree that shelters you.
—Danish proverb

Rhubarb Soup
Rabarbersuppe

Julie Jensen McDonald

12 stalks rhubarb (about 2
  pounds)
1 stick cinnamon
  juice of 1/2 lemon
1 cup sugar (more if desired)
2 tablespoons cornstarch

Cut rhubarb into 1-inch lengths and cook in enough water to cover until tender. Strain and discard pulp. Reheat juice. Add cinnamon and lemon juice. Add sugar. Thicken with cornstarch mixed with a little water.

Serve with pumpernickel or rusks. This is good hot or cold and a fine way to use up the rhubarb offered by kind friends.

Variation: Gooseberries or cherries may be substituted for the rhubarb, and they take about half as much sugar.

Fruit Sago Soup
Sagosuppe

Myrtle Petersen, Harlan, Iowa, mother of the author. "Sagosuppe is one of the happy taste memories of my childhood. It's good either hot or cold," Julie recalls.

8 cups water
1/2 cup sago or
  1/3 cup minute tapioca
1 stick cinnamon
1 cup prunes
1/2 cup raisins
1/2 cup fruit juice, peach or
  pear
1/4 cup sugar

Bring water to a boil; add sago, cinnamon stick, prunes, and raisins. Simmer until sago is clear. Add juice and sugar. More juice or sugar may be added to taste. Serves eight.

You may light
another's candle
with your own
without loss.
—Danish proverb

Breads

Among my fondest memories are the images of my grandmother and my mother kneading and shaping bread and rolls, the heavenly aroma of baking day and the first marvelous bite from a golden or dark brown loaf of bread fresh from the oven. At a very early age, I decided that Danish women have a way with everything that rises, and baking is my own favorite adventure in food preparation.

The Danes are famous for *smørrebrød,* the open-faced sandwiches that make the most of the national breads with great artistry. The bread, however, becomes the silent partner. As one *smørrebrød* expert insists, "Everything on the top must hang over the side so that no bread shows." In Denmark and other places where Danes are numerous, the staff of life can be earthy, sophisticated, or both, but it always discourages stopping at one slice.

Tricks from Vienna

In the late 1860s, the bakers of Copenhagen went on strike, demanding cash wages rather than the traditional room and board. Their employers replaced them with Germans and Austrians, but eventually the Danes returned to their jobs. They picked up the tricks of the Vienna bakers, improved upon them by adding jams and fillings, and voilà—*wienerbrød!* Even the Austrians were impressed.

Old-fashioned Clove Bread
Gammeldags Nellike Brød

Birte Lund, Funen, Denmark

2 cups lukewarm milk
2 tablespoons yeast
2 teaspoons salt
1/3 cup maple syrup
4 tablespoons oil
2 teaspoons ground cloves
4-1/2 to 5 cups whole wheat flour, or half unbleached white and half whole wheat flour
milk for brushing
poppy seed for top

Dissolve yeast in milk. Add remaining ingredients and knead dough thoroughly. Let rise in a warm place for about 15 minutes. Divide the dough in two parts and roll in 20-inch lengths. Twist together the long rolls. Let rise about 20 minutes. Brush with milk, sprinkle with poppy seed, and bake on a greased cookie sheet at 375° about 45 minutes, depending on the oven.

This is a hearty, heavy bread that is good with plenty of butter.

Judge a maiden
at the kneading trough,
not at the dance.
—Danish proverb

Sourdough Pumpernickel
Dansk Rugbrød

Eleanor Petersen, Davenport, Iowa

1 cake yeast
1/4 cup lukewarm water
   sourdough (see below)
1/4 cup salt
6 cups lukewarm water
4 cups rye graham or white
   flour
12 cups rye meal

Dissolve yeast in 1/4 cup water. Mix the yeast, sourdough, salt, 6 cups water, and the flours. Mix well and let rise for 2 hours. Knead dough and let it stand for 15 minutes. Shape into loaves and let the dough rise again for about 20 minutes. Bake at 375° for 1-1/2 to 1-3/4 hours. Makes three 2-1/2 pound loaves.

Sourdough:
1 cup yeast dough of any kind
2-1/2 cups lukewarm water
1/2 cup rye meal

The sourdough *(Surdej)* is made by blending yeast dough with lukewarm water and rye meal and letting it stand overnight at room temperature.

Esther's Danish Rye Bread
Dansk Rugbrød

Esther Andersen, Dike, Iowa

1 teaspoon yeast
1/4 cup warm water
1 quart buttermilk
3 tablespoons molasses
3 tablespoons lard
3 tablespoons salt
6 cups rye graham flour
6 cups whole wheat flour

Soften yeast in warm water. Heat buttermilk until lukewarm. Mix all ingredients and knead. Let stand overnight, covered. Punch down in the morning. Divide into 3 loaves and let rise in 9 x 5-inch loaf pans 10 minutes. Place cookie sheet over pans with a weight on top while baking. Bake at 400° for 10 minutes, then at 250° for 1-3/4 hours. Bread must be sliced very thin for serving. This bread is excellent for open-faced sandwiches.

Mardeen's Danish Rye Bread
Dansk Rugbrød

Mardeen Petersen, whose husband is Danish, is from Long Grove, IA

1 orange, including peel
3/4 cup plus 1 teaspoon sugar, divided
1 cake or package dry yeast
1/3 cup lukewarm water
1 tablespoon salt
1 teaspoon anise seed
1/2 cup vegetable oil
1/2 cup molasses
2 cups rye flour
10 cups white flour, divided
1 egg white, slightly beaten

Squeeze orange and set juice aside. Cut orange peel finely and combine with 1/2 cup sugar and enough water to cover. Cook and set aside to cool. Dissolve yeast in 1/3 cup lukewarm water along with 1 teaspoon sugar. Set aside. Mix 1/4 cup sugar, orange juice mixed with enough hot water to make 3 cups, salt, anise seed, oil, molasses, rye flour, and 3 cups of white flour. Add yeast mixture and mix thoroughly. Add remaining white flour a cup at a time, mixing after each addition. Knead at least 15 minutes. Place in a greased bowl and lightly oil top of dough. Let rise until double or overnight for sour bread.

Oil hands and form dough into 4 round loaves. When not quite double, cut groove about 1/8 to 1/4-inch deep. Beat a little egg white and brush some on top of each loaf. Bake at 375° for 15 minutes, then at 350° for 30 to 45 minutes.

Windmill Danish Rye Bread
Dansk Rugbrød

Minna Larsen, who immigrated to Audubon County, Iowa, when she was only 12 years old was always proud of her Danish roots, but she was so ever proud of being an American. She was known to bake 40 loaves at a time. She loved the windmill rye as it included the graham in the flour.

8 cups warm water
1/2 cup lard
1/2 cup sugar or molasses
8 teaspoons salt
2 packages of yeast in 1/2 cup warm water
8 cups graham flour
8 cups windmill rye flour
8 cups white flour, approximately

Combine water, lard, sugar, and salt. Add yeast mixture. Add graham flour and beat well. Add rye flour and as much white flour to make a firm dough. Let rise until double bulk. Knead dough and form in loaves. Let loaves rise in greased bread pans. Bake at 350° for 1 hour. Makes 8–10 loaves depending on size.

You must bake
with the flour you have.
—Danish proverb

Anna's Rye Bread
Sigtebrød

Anna Nielsen, Solvang, California

2 cups milk
2 tablespoons shortening
1/2 cup brown sugar
2 cups rye flour
1 tablespoon salt
2 cakes yeast dissolved in 1/2
    cup warm water
6 cups white flour

Scald milk. Add shortening and brown sugar and cool. Add rye flour, salt, and yeast. Add approximately six cups flour, enough to make a stiff dough. Let rise until double, about three hours. Knead and form into two loaves. Bake at 425° 15 minutes, then at 325° for 35 minutes.

Lenten Rolls
Fastelavnsboller

Anna Nielsen, Solvang, California

1-1/2 cups milk, scalded
1/2 cup butter or margarine
1/3 cup sugar
1 teaspoon salt
2 well beaten eggs
1 package yeast, dissolved in
    1/4 cup lukewarm water
2 cups flour
1 cup raisins
1/3 cup chopped citron
1/2 teaspoon ground cardamom
2-1/2 more cups flour

Combine first seven ingredients and beat until bubbly. Add raisins, citron, and cardamom. Add 2-1/2 cups flour. Knead well, place in greased bowl, and let rise until double. Form into small balls and let rise until light. Brush with butter. Bake 15 to 20 minutes at 375°. When baked, put on a powdered sugar glaze.

Walnut Wreaths
Valnøddekrans

Birte Lund, Funen, Denmark

1 cup boiling water
2/3 cup whole wheat flour
2 tablespoons yeast
1/4 cup lukewarm water
1 tablespoon salt
1 tablespoon corn syrup
1 cup yogurt
3 ounces coarsely chopped
    walnuts
3-1/2 cups unbleached white flour

First pour boiling water over whole wheat flour and let sit for several hours. Dissolve yeast in lukewarm water. Stir it plus the salt, syrup, yogurt, walnuts, and unbleached flour into the whole wheat and water mix. Knead dough thoroughly. Let rise in a warm place for about 45 minutes. Punch the dough down and divide into two parts. Roll each portion into a long stick, twine the sticks and shape them into a wreath. Let rise again for about 15 minutes. Preheat oven to 375° and bake for about 35 minutes.

Country Crust Bread
Landbrød

Elisabeth Wood, Rock Island, Illinois, whose parents were born in Denmark

2 cups water
1/2 cup sugar
1 teaspoon salt
1/4 cup oil
2 eggs, beaten
2 packages dry yeast
6-1/2 to 7-1/2 cups unbleached flour, divided

Heat water, sugar, salt, and oil to lukewarm. Add the beaten eggs and yeast. With electric beater or spoon, beat in half of the flour until smooth. Then add rest of flour gradually until it does not stick to the bowl. (If a bread mixer is used, add everything after the water is heated. Add the flour gradually until dough leaves sides of container.) Let rise until double in bulk. Knead down and divide dough in half. Press each half out on a greased board or counter. Roll up from small end and put seam-side down in a greased loaf pan. Bake at 375° for 35 minutes. Makes 2 loaves.

Everyday Buns
Grove Boller

Birte Lund, Funen, Denmark, writes, "Many young Danes are health food conscious these days, and these buns are rich in fiber."

4 tablespoons yeast
1/3 cup lukewarm water
4 tablespoons olive oil, warmed
2-1/3 cups yogurt
1/3 cup soy flour
1/3 cup bran
2 tablespoons sea salt
2 tablespoons flax seed
1-2/3 cups whole wheat flour
3/4 cup rye flour
3-1/4 cups unbleached flour, divided
1/3 cup raisins
1/3 cup chopped hazelnuts

Stir yeast in water and mix with lukewarm oil and yogurt. Add remaining ingredients except filberts, raisins, and 1/3 cup unbleached flour. Knead dough and let rise to double its size. Add raisins, nuts, and remaining 1/3 cup unbleached flour and knead again. Shape into about 40 buns and let rise for one-half hour on greased cookie sheet. Bake 15 minutes at 375°.

When there is room in the heart
there is room in the house.
—Danish proverb

Pastries

What most Americans recognize as a "Danish" is heavier and soggier than the real thing, which melts like a morning dream at the first touch of the teeth. Shakespeare borrowed a real Danish prince named Amleth for Hamlet, and the Danes know how to borrow with just as much discrimination. That's why Danish pastry is called *wienerbrød*, literally, "Vienna bread."

Danish Doughnuts
Æbleskiver

Hulda Sorensen, LeClaire, Iowa

2 cups flour
1/2 teaspoon salt
1 teaspoon sugar
2 cups buttermilk
2 eggs, separated
1 teaspoon baking soda
melted butter
jelly or applesauce

Mix flour, salt, and sugar. Beat together buttermilk and egg yolks, and add the flour mixture. Add soda and fold in stiffly beaten egg whites. Heat the pan and put melted butter in each hole in pan. Pour batter into holes, but do not quite fill them. Place over low heat and turn quickly when half done. Serve very hot with jelly or applesauce.

Note: Danish doughnuts are baked on top of the stove in a special pan with a hole for each doughnut. *Æbleskiver* pans may be purchased at most Scandinavian specialty or gourmet cookware shops.

Danish Pancakes
Bedstemors Æbleskiver

This recipe is a Sunday morning favorite in the home of Thora Mae Andersen, Solvang, California. "What is great about this recipe is that it's so easy to increase, whether it be up to a half, double, etc."

2 eggs, separated
1 cup flour
2 teaspoons baking powder
1/4 teaspoon salt
1 cup milk

Separate eggs and beat whites until stiff. Sift dry ingredients. Add egg yolks and milk to dry ingredients and beat until smooth. Fold in egg whites.

Put about one tablespoon shortening in the bottom of each *æbleskiver* pan and heat. Fill holes completely with batter and as soon as they get bubbly around the edge, turn quickly. A knitting needle or fork may be used for turning. Continue cooking, turning the ball to keep it from burning. The fork or needle will come out clean from the center when done.

Serve while hot with syrup, jam, or sugar. Makes approximately 18.

Danish Doughnuts #2
Æbleskiver

This recipe is from Old World Wisconsin, the outdoor living history museum in Kettle Moraine State Forest near Eagle, Wisconsin.

3 eggs, separated
1/2 teaspoon salt
2 cups buttermilk
2 cups sifted flour
1 teaspoon baking soda
1 teaspoon baking powder
butter
confectioner's sugar, granulated sugar, brown sugar, jelly, jam, applesauce, butter, or maple syrup

Combine in mixing bowl: 3 egg yolks, salt, buttermilk, and beat well. Then add sifted flour, baking soda, and baking powder. Beat egg whites until stiff and add to batter. Heat æbleskiver pan and put a small amount of butter in each of seven baking cups. Fill each cup 2/3 full of batter and fry until bubbly on top, then turn and fry the bottom. Serve hot, dusted with confectioner's sugar or dipped in one of the other sweet condiments listed above. *See note

Water Pretzel
Vandkringle

Eleanor Petersen, Davenport, Iowa

3/4 cup butter
1 cup warmed whole milk
1 cake yeast
4 cups flour
1/2 cup sugar
3 eggs
1 teaspoon cardamon
raisins, citron and salt to taste
sugar for sprinkling
sliced almonds

Melt butter in warmed milk. Cool. Dissolve yeast in cool milk. Mix in remaining ingredients except sugar and almonds, and beat about 15 minutes. Mixture should slip from the spoon. Sift flour onto a clean dish towel and pour dough on it. Gather towel and tie with string. Place in cold water deep enough to cover. Let set overnight.

Handling as little as possible, form dough into a pretzel shape. Sprinkle generously with sugar and sliced almonds and let rise about 2 hours or until light. Bake 30 minutes at 400°. Makes one large pretzel.

*Editor's note: These round doughnuts were favorite treats on Sundays or holidays, and at Danish festivals. Danish women used wooden knitting needles to turn the æbleskivers.

Danish Puff
Vandbakkelse

Betty Schutter, Algona, Iowa

1 cup butter or margarine,
    divided
2 cups flour, divided
1/4 teaspoon salt
2 tablespoons cold water
1 cup boiling water
1 teaspoon almond flavoring
3 eggs

Frosting:
1-1/2 cups sifted powdered sugar
1 tablespoon butter
3 tablespoons cream
1 teaspoon vanilla
1/8 teaspoon salt

Cut 1/2 cup of the butter into 1 cup of flour and salt to a consistency of coarse meal. Add cold water and blend well. Divide dough in half and press each half onto an ungreased cookie sheet.

Pour boiling water into saucepan and add remaining half cup of butter. When butter melts, remove from heat and add flavoring. Stir in 1 cup of flour all at once. Beat smooth and let cool. Add 1 egg at a time, beating well after each addition. Spread this mixture over the pastry on the cookie sheet. Bake at 425° for 15 minutes, then at 400° for 30 to 35 minutes longer. Watch closely.

Mix frosting ingredients together until smooth and spreadable. Frost while hot, slice, and serve warm.

This puff should be paraded proudly before your guests just as it comes out of the oven looking like a beautiful, golden cloud. Then you can frost it and add candy, nuts, or fruit garnish for an encore.

Grandma's Coffee Cake
Bedstemors Kaffekage

Esther Andersen, Dike, Iowa

2 packages yeast
1/4 cup warm water
1 cup milk
1/2 cup butter
1/2 cup sugar
1 teaspoon salt
2 eggs, beaten
1 teaspoon ground cardamom
4-1/2 cups flour (approximately)
    butter
    sugar
    raisins or candied fruit

Soften yeast in warm water. Scald milk; add butter, sugar, and salt. Add beaten eggs. Cool to lukewarm. Add yeast, fresh ground cardamom, and flour. Beat well. Let rise until double. Roll out and spread with softened butter. Sprinkle with sugar and raisins or candied fruit. Roll, place in buttered pan. Slash top, brush with soft butter, and sprinkle with sugar. Let rise and bake at 350° for 45 minutes.

Danish Twists
Dansk Flætbrød

Esther Andersen, Dike, Iowa

1 package yeast
1/4 cup warm water
3-1/2 cups flour
1 teaspoon salt
1 cup margarine
1 cup sour cream
2 egg yolks
1 teaspoon vanilla

Sugar filling:
1-1/2 cups sugar
3 teaspoons vanilla

Soften yeast in lukewarm water. Mix flour, salt, and margarine like pie crust. Add sour cream, yeast, egg yolks, and vanilla. Refrigerate overnight. Roll out half the dough into a 14 x 12-inch rectangle. Mix sugar and vanilla for filling. Place 1/4 cup sugar filling on 2/3 of the dough. Fold into thirds and roll again. Repeat 2 times, using sugar on the board the last time. Fold into rectangle 4 inches wide and cut into strips. Twist and place on buttered cookie sheet to rise. Repeat with rest of dough. Bake at 350° for 15 minutes.

Danish Pastry with Fruit Strips
Dansk Wienerbrød med Frugt

Esther Emilie Thuesen Andersen earned her reputation as a peerless cook in Fredsville, Iowa.

4 cups flour
4 tablespoons sugar
1-1/2 cups margarine
1/2 teaspoon salt
2 packages yeast
1/3 cup warm water
4 egg yolks, beaten
2/3 cup evaporated milk

Filling:
4 egg whites, beaten
brown sugar
prune, almond, or cherry
  filling
sugar
slivered almonds for topping

Mix first four ingredients like pie crust. Soften yeast in warm water. Add to flour mixture. Combine egg yolks and milk and add to flour mixture. Beat well. Refrigerate overnight.

Divide dough into 6 parts and roll out thin. Spread each with beaten egg whites mixed with a little brown sugar. Put fruit filling down the centers and fold in sides. Brush tops with egg white mixture. Sprinkle with sugar and top with slivered almonds. Let rise 1 to 2 hours and bake at 350° for 20 minutes. Makes 6 pastries.

O&H *Kringle*

O&H Danish Bakery, Racine, Wisconsin

This recipe for two kringles *in proportions for the housewife is courtesy of Ray and Mryna Olesen of Racine, Wisconsin. The Olesens use no preservatives in their* kringles *and fillings. The filling enhances the flavor and prevents the fruit from soaking into the pastry. Pecan is the most popular filling along with cherry, apple, and almond close behind. "The minimum of 32 layers of dough folded over butter is what makes this Danish pastry," says Ray Olesen. "This is what is different from just a sweet dough. To make* kringle *correctly is virtually an all-day project at home. For the best results, you cannot deviate from the procedure." The Olesens ship* kringles *all over America, as do several other bakeries in Racine.*

Photo from O&H Danish Bakery
O&H Danish Bakery's
pecan kringle

Kringle dough:
   3/4 cup butter
   1 package or cake yeast
   1/4 cup warm water
   1/4 cup lukewarm milk
   1/4 cup sugar
   1/2 teaspoon salt
   1/2 teaspoon lemon extract
   1 egg
   2 cups sifted all-purpose flour

Divide butter in half and spread each half on waxed paper to an 8 x 8-inch square. Chill.

Dissolve yeast in warm water. Add lukewarm milk, sugar, salt, lemon extract, and egg, mixing well. Add flour and mix until smooth.

Roll dough on well-floured board to an 8 x 12-inch rectangle. Place one piece of chilled butter on two thirds of dough. Fold uncovered third of dough over the middle third, then fold the remaining third over the top. Again fold one end over middle third, and fold remaining third layer over top, making a square of nine layers. Wrap in waxed paper and refrigerate 30 minutes.

Roll dough again to an 8 x 12-inch rectangle. Add chilled butter and fold the same way. This makes 18 layers. Refrigerate 2 hours.

Cut dough into two equal pieces. Lightly roll one piece at a time, until piece is about 20 by 6 inches. Spread center third of dough with butterscotch filling (right), then add fruit, nuts, raisins, and so on, or fill with jam. Fold one of the long edges to the middle, moisten other edge and fold over the top to cover filling. Seal well. Put *kringle* on greased baking sheet and form into oval shape, pressing ends of *kringle* together to form a continuous circle. Flatten dough with hands. Cover *kringle* for one hour at 70°. Bake at 350° for 25 to 30 minutes or until golden brown. Cool, then ice with mixture of powdered sugar and water.

Butterscotch Filling for Two *Kringles:*
   1 cup brown sugar
   1/3 cup butter
      pinch of salt
      pinch of cinnamon
   1/2 egg white

Mix until smooth.

Kringles keep very well in the freezer, or for several days in the refrigerator. The high butter content keeps them moist.

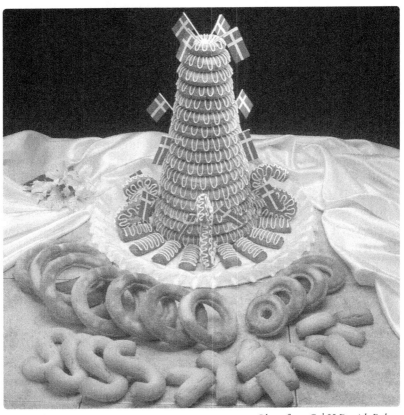

Photo from O&H Danish Bakery

Danish kransekrager *from O&H Danish Bakery*
Racine, Wisconsin

—151

Irene's Danish *Kringle*
Dansk Kringle

This recipe is from Irene Jessen Olson of Story City, Iowa, who is a retired school teacher. She is a collector of Danish recipes and is president of the Iowa-Minnesota United Lodges of the Danish Sisterhood. "This is good for afternoon coffee. We always serve it for Christmas breakfast."

1 package yeast
1/4 cup warm milk
1 cup butter or margarine
2-1/4 cups flour
1 teaspoon salt
2 tablespoons sugar
2 eggs, beaten

Filling:
1/2 cup butter
1/2 cup sugar
fruit filling as desired
vanilla or almond extract
egg white
nuts, if desired

Dissolve yeast in warm milk. Mix butter or margarine, flour, and salt as for pie crust. Add the yeast and sugar. Add as much of beaten eggs as you need to absorb the flour mixture. Turn onto a floured board and knead until smooth. Divide into 2 or 3 parts and roll each into oblong strips.

Cream butter and sugar together and spread on strips of dough. Spread with desired fruit filling, to which flavoring has been added. Fold into thirds lengthwise and place on a greased baking sheet, seam side up. Brush with beaten egg white and sprinkle with nuts or leave plain and frost later. Let rise for 2 hours. Bake for 20 minutes at 350° to 375°. Slice into strips 1 to 1-1/2 inches wide.

Marjorie's Danish *Kringle*
Dansk Kringle

Marjorie K. Severtson, Albert Lea, Minnesota

3 cups flour
1 cup butter or margarine
1 cup cream
pinch of salt
1 teaspoon baking powder
2 teaspoons sugar
2 teaspoons vanilla

Mix all ingredients as for pie crust. Roll out thin, about 1/4-inch, and cut into 1/4-inch strips. Shape like a figure 8 and dip top side into sugar. Place on an ungreased cookie sheet. Bake at 350° until lightly browned. Cool cookie sheets each time before baking next part of dough.

Desserts

And for anyone who has a Danish streak, a dinner with no dessert is a romance with no kisses. Danes love their sweets. They want them to look good, taste good, and be good—produced from the finest ingredients.

The most glamorous dessert I have ever consumed was created in a Copenhagen restaurant. It was a dream of ice cream, whipped cream, and fresh fruit served in a molded chocolate cup and sprinkled with candied violets. This triumph of the Danish culinary imagination was called Cleopatra.

Here's sugar and spice and everything nice in the Danish manner.

Danish Butter Cookies
Danske Smørkager

Olive Scotland Ferguson, Walnut, Iowa

1-1/4 cups butter
1-1/2 cups sugar
3 egg yolks, unbeaten
2-1/4 cups sifted white flour
1 teaspoon soda
1 teaspoon cream of tartar
1-1/2 teaspoons almond flavoring

Thoroughly cream butter and sugar. Beat in egg yolks, one at a time. Add remaining ingredients, mix, and chill in a covered bowl. Roll dough into small round balls and place on ungreased cookie sheet. Press dough with any press dipped in sugar. Bake at 325° for 12 to 15 minutes. Remove immediately from cookie sheet. Makes 2-1/2 dozen.

Countess Cookies
Grevinde Småkager

Esther Andersen, Dike, Iowa

1 cup vegetable shortening
1/4 cup butter
3/4 cup brown sugar
1 egg, beaten
2 teaspoons vanilla
1-1/2 cups flour
1-1/4 teaspoons baking powder
3/4 teaspoon salt
quick-cooking oatmeal
maraschino cherries

Mix ingredients except oatmeal and cherries in order given. Moisten hands and shape dough into small balls. Roll in quick-cooking oatmeal, making as much as possible stick to the dough. Place on greased cookie sheet. Cut maraschino cherries into quarters, then crosswise, pressing one piece into each cookie. Bake at 350° for 12 minutes.

Danish Cones
Kræmmerhuse

This recipe comes from Ellen Madison, Bettendorf, Iowa, who was national president of the Danish Sisterhood of America from 1964 to 1970. Mrs. Madison's father, John Hansen, was knighted by the Danish King (Frederik IX) for his contribution to Danish war relief in the wake of World War II.

1/2 cup margarine
1/2 cup sugar
1 scant cup flour
4 egg whites, beaten stiff

Soften margarine and stir in sugar. Add flour and then egg whites beaten very stiff. Grease a cookie sheet well and place on it teaspoonfuls of dough with considerable space between (only four to a cookie sheet). Flatten each pat of dough to an oblong shape with a spoon. Bake quickly in 450° oven for 5 minutes or until lightly browned. Pull pan half out of oven and take off one cake at a time. Form into a cone while warm. Shape around a wooden spoon handle. As pastry cools, it becomes crisp and cannot be formed. Handle with extreme care.

Place in a container until ready to serve, then fill with whipped cream, adding a pat of jelly on the top (currant, strawberry, or raspberry).

This recipe makes about 35 cones. They are spectacular poked into a heaping bowl of white sugar for a banquet effect. The cones may be served as dessert or just with coffee.

Smalls
Ægte Danske Klejner

Mrs. Evelyn Hansen Behrens, Albert Lea, Minnesota

6 egg yolks
2 whole eggs
1 cup sugar
1 teaspoon salt
2 tablespoons cream
1 tablespoon butter, melted
4 cups flour

Beat egg yolks, eggs, sugar, and salt. Add cream, butter, and enough flour to make a batter stiff enough to roll out like cookies. Cut in diamond shapes, make slit lengthwise in center, and put one end through slit. Cook in deep hot fat until light brown. Cook only 6 to 8 at a time, turning with a fork or knitting needle.

by Esther Feske

Danish Fruit Drop Cookies
Danske Frugt Småkager

From Lehmann's Bakery co-founder, Judy Carlson, Racine, Wisconsin

1/2 cup plus 2 tablespoons shortening
1/2 cup plus 2 tablespoons butter
2 cups brown sugar, no lumps
2 very large eggs
5 cups flour
2 teaspoons salt
2-1/2 teaspoons baking soda
1/2 cup plus 2 tablespoons sour
milk
2 cups chopped pecans
1/2 cup plus 2 tablespoons
candied cherries, halved
1 cup plus 2 tablespoons
coarsely cut dates, pecan
halves or other nuts or dried
fruit for garnish

Cream shortening and butter and gradually add sugar. Cream thoroughly. Add eggs one at a time, beating lightly. Sift flour, salt, and soda. Add alternately with milk. Add chopped pecans, candied cherries, and dates, mixing enough to have a smooth dough. Drop by teaspoonfuls on a greased cookie sheet. Place half a pecan on each cookie. Additional fruit or other fruit may be added such as raisins, citron, candied pineapple, hazelnuts, or almonds. (Lehmann's Bakery uses candied pineapple and cherries.) Bake 10 to 12 minutes at 375°. Makes about 8 dozen cookies.

Peppernuts
Pebernødder

Julie Jensen-McDonald relates, "This recipe belonged to the late Rigmor Sondergaard, Harlan, Iowa, and my mother has the patience to make them for me every Christmas. They're tiny cookies, but some people mistake them for nuts on a festive table."

1 cup butter
1-1/3 scant cups sugar
2 eggs
4 cups flour
1 teaspoon soda
1 teaspoon ground ginger
1/2 teaspoon anise extract
1/4 teaspoon nutmeg
1/2 teaspoon salt
1/2 teaspoon cinnamon
1/2 cup sorghum
1/2 teaspoon vanilla

Work all ingredients together and roll into tiny balls about the size of a nickel. Put on cookie sheet. Bake 9–10 minutes in a 300° oven. Quantity depends on size. My mother fills two half-gallon containers from this recipe.

Dagmar Jensen of Clinton, Iowa, also sent a similar *pebernødder.*

He who tickles himself,

laughs when he pleases.

—Danish proverb

Square Peppernuts
Pebernødder

Joan Madsen Meier, Geneseo, Illinois, says, "My grandmother, who came from Denmark, always made these rich, butter pastry squares for Christmas."

    1/2 cup sugar
      1 cup butter (do not use margarine)
      2 cups flour
    3/8 teaspoon black pepper
      1 teaspoon baking powder
      1 generous tablespoon milk (just enough for stiff pie dough consistency)

Cream sugar and butter. Add sifted dry ingredients and cut in as in making pie crust. Add milk while tossing pastry with fork. Make as stiff as possible. Form into several balls with hands and roll each ball into a rectangle about 1/8-inch thick. Using a table knife, cut into 3/4-inch squares. Place squares on cookie sheet and bake at 425° until just slightly brown (about 6 or 7 minutes). Watch closely, as they burn easily.

> An unpleasant guest
> is as welcome as
> salt to a sore eye.
> —Danish proverb

Filled Cookies
Fyldte Småkager

Julie Jensen-McDonald: "I remember getting a box of these cookies when I was six and in the hospital. Nothing ever tasted better."

      1 cup sugar
      1 cup shortening
      1 egg
    2/3 cup milk
      1 teaspoon vanilla
      2 teaspoons cream of tartar
      1 teaspoon baking soda
      2 to 4 cups flour

Cream sugar and shortening; add egg and milk. Add vanilla. Mix cream of tartar, soda, and 2 cups flour, combining with first mixture. Add flour to rolling consistency. Roll as thin as possible on floured board, and cut with small, round cookie cutter. Bake to light brown at 350°. Put two cookies together with filling before they cool.

Vanilla Wreaths or Spritz
Vanillakranse

From Dana College, Blair, Nebraska

    1-1/2 cups butter
  2-1/4 cups sugar
      2 eggs, beaten
  1-1/2 teaspoons vanilla
  3-1/2 cups flour
    1/2 cup finely chopped almonds

Cream butter and sugar. Add the rest of the ingredients. Mix until dough is smooth. Put dough in cookie press and press out onto greased cookie sheet in small wreaths (1-1/2-inch diameter). Bake at 325° until slightly brown. Makes approximately 150.

Cream Wafers
Flødevafler

Olive Scotland Ferguson, Walnut, IA

Wafers:
- 1 cup soft butter
- 2 cups sifted white flour
- 1/3 cup thick sweet cream

Filling:
- 1/2 cup soft butter
- 1-1/2 cups powdered sugar
- 2 egg yolks (unbeaten)
- 1-1/2 teaspoons vanilla

Wafers: Mix all ingredients together and chill in a covered bowl. Working with a little dough at a time, roll the mixture into small balls. (Continue to refrigerate remaining dough.) Place balls on ungreased cookie sheet and press down to 1/4-inch thickness. Sprinkle with sugar, prick with a fork, and bake 10 minutes at 325°.

Filling: Combine ingredients and beat well. Put two wafers together with filling between.

These cookies freeze well.

Coconut Haloes
Kokoskranse

The Danish Sisterhood News, *edited by Hazel G. Smith, Racine, WI*

- 1 cup butter
- 1 cup sugar
- 2 eggs, beaten
- 1/2 teaspoon vanilla
- 2-1/2 scant cups flour
- 2 teaspoons baking powder
- 1/2 cup grated coconut
- 1/2 cup finely ground almonds

Cream butter and sugar. Stir in beaten eggs and vanilla. Sift flour and baking powder together. Combine with creamed mixture. Add grated coconut and almonds. Force through cookie press and shape into small wreaths. Bake at 350° to 375° until done.

Filling:
- 1 cup raisins, chopped
- 1 cup water
- 1 cup sugar
- 2 teaspoons flour
- 1/2 cup chopped nuts

Cook the first four ingredients together about 10 minutes, or until thick. Cool. Add chopped nuts. Join cookies so top sides are out.

Danish Shortbread
Dansk Brød

Danish Agricultural Producers

1/2 pound butter
3/4 cup plus 2 tablespoons powdered sugar, sifted
2 cups white flour
2 cups corn flour
1 egg yolk

Beat butter and sifted sugar until light and fluffy. Gradually mix in sifted flour and corn flour and bind with egg yolk. Roll out to a 9-inch circle on a lightly greased baking sheet. Crimp edges, mark into 8 or 10 wedges and prick the shortbread all over with a fork. Bake in a 350° oven for 1 hour or until golden brown.

Finnish Shortbread
Finsk Brød

*The former Dana College
Blair, Nebraska*

4 cups flour
pinch of salt
1 cup sugar
2 cups butter
1 beaten egg
chopped almonds
1 tablespoon sugar

Sift flour; add salt, sugar and butter. Knead. Roll in long slender rolls 1/2" in diameter. Cut in 1-1/2" lengths. Dip each cookie in beaten egg; then dip in mixture of chopped almonds and small amount of sugar. Bake at 375° until slightly brown. Makes approximately 150.

Apple Bars
Æblesnitter

Beverly Manske, a seventh grade teacher in Algona, Iowa. According to Penny Davidsen of Iowa City, cornflakes were exported to Denmark almost as soon as they were made available to Americans.

2-1/2 cups flour
1 teaspoon salt
1 tablespoon sugar
1 cup shortening
2 egg yolks, slightly beaten
scant 2/3 cup milk
1-1/2 cups cornflakes
8 to 10 apples, sliced
1-1/2 cups sugar mixed with
1-1/4 teaspoons cinnamon
2 egg whites
thin powdered sugar frosting

Sift the flour, salt, and tablespoon of sugar together. Cut in the cup of shortening. Put egg yolks in measuring cup and add milk to the 2/3 level. Combine flour and egg mixtures. Pat half the dough into a 15 x 10-inch pan. Sprinkle on cornflakes. Add the thinly sliced apples and sprinkle them with cinnamon-sugar mixture. Roll out the rest of the dough for the top crust and bind edges together around apples. Beat egg whites until frothy and spread over crust. Bake 50 minutes at 350°. Drizzle powdered sugar frosting over the top crust.

Dessert Royal
Kongelig Dessert

Birte Lund, Funen, Denmark

4 bananas
4 tablespoons Chartreuse
  liqueur
3/4 cup whipping cream,
  whipped
4 tablespoons strawberries,
  frozen or fresh

Cut the bananas in slices. Soak them in Chartreuse for 10 minutes. Arrange the banana slices in serving glasses, cover with whipped cream, and top with strawberries.

This recipe serves four and is a delicious way to display the Danish national colors, red and white.

Apple Cake (Version #1)
Æblekage

Elisabeth Wood, Rock Island, IL

2 cups crumbs (bread, cake, or
  combination)
1 tablespoon sugar
1/2 cup butter
2-1/2 cups tart applesauce
1 cup whipping cream
2 tablespoons sugar
  red jelly or jam for decoration

Brown crumbs in skillet with 1 tablespoon sugar and butter. Arrange crumb mixture and applesauce in alternate layers in glass serving dish. Chill in refrigerator. Whip the cream with 2 tablespoons sugar for topping and decorate with dabs of jelly.

For a crunchy texture, serve immediately after preparation. Advance preparation will create a moist blend of layers. This cake looks elegant served in a crystal 1-1/2 or 2-quart bowl.

Apple Cake (Version #2)
Æblekage

Hulda Sorensen of LeClaire, Iowa, enjoys this recipe from Denmark.

2 pounds cooking apples
  sugar
  vanilla
  dried bread crumbs
1 cup melted butter
  jelly
  whipped cream

Peel, quarter, and core apples. In a covered pan, simmer apples in a little water until soft. Force through a sieve and sweeten to taste. Add vanilla to taste.

Butter an oven-proof dish. Put layers of bread crumbs and layers of applesauce in the dish alternately, making the bottom and top layers bread crumbs. Pour the melted butter down through the layers and bake for 30 minutes on a hot oven. Turn onto a plate and decorate with jelly and whipped cream.

Additional whipped cream may be served in a separate dish. Serve either hot or cold.

Danish Layer Cake #1
Dansk Lagkage

*O&H Danish Bakery
Racine, Wisconsin*

1 cup butter
2 cups granulated sugar
3 eggs
3 cups sifted cake flour
1 tablespoon baking powder
1-1/4 cups milk
1 teaspoon vanilla

Cream butter than gradually add sugar and beat well. Add eggs, one at a time, beating well after each addition. In another bowl sift the flour and add the baking powder. In another bowl combine the milk and the vanilla. Add approximately half the flour; blend, mix until incorporated. Add half of the milk; blend, mix until incorprated. Repeat. Mix well. Pour batter into 2 greased and floured 9" pans. Bake at 350° for approximately 25 minutes or until a toothpick inserted in the center comes out clean. Cool in pan for 10 minutes, flip the pans onto a wax paper lined cookie sheet and cool completely.

Custard Cream Filling:
2 cups whole milk
2/3 cup sugar
1/2 cup flour
pinch salt
2 eggs, well beaten
1 teaspoon vanilla
1 tablespoon butter

In a 4-quart sauce pan, scald the milk, being careful not to burn. Mix together sugar, flour, and salt. Add eggs to flour mixture and beat well. Add the egg/flour mixture slowly to scalding milk, stirring constantly with whisk until thick. It will thicken rapidly. Remove from heat and add vanilla and butter. Stir and cool.

Raspberry Filling:
1-1/2 cups frozen rapsberries
1 tablespoon cornstarch
2 tablespoons lemon juice
1/4 cup granulated sugar

In a small sauce pan, combine all ingredients and slowly bring to a boil over medium-high heat (keep stirring until thickened for best results.) Let cool completely before spreading onto the cake.

Buttercream frosting:
1 cup butter at room temperature
3-1/2 cups sifted confectioner's (powdered) sugar
1/4 teaspoon salt
1 tablespoon vanilla extract
1/4 cup heavy cream

Beat butter for a few minutes with a mixer and paddle attachment on medium speed until smooth with no lumps. Turn mixer to low speed and add the powdered sugar slowly (so the sugar doesn't blow everywhere) until the sugar has been incorporated with the butter. Increase mixer speed to medium and add vanilla extract and salt, blending for five minutes. Pour 1/2 of the cream in the bowl and turn on the mixer momentarily to mix in just a portion of the liquid. Turn off mixer and scrape down the bowl. Turn mixer to high speed and thread in very slowly the remaining cream. Mix five additional minutes at high speed. During this step, if your frosting needs a more stiff consistency, you may add additional sugar. If your frosting needs to be softer, add additional cream 1 tablespoon at a time.

To Assemble Danish Layer Cake:

After the two cakes have cooled, cut each into two, making four layers. Place the first layer on your platter, spread on a layer of cooled custard. Then spread a cooled thin layer of raspberry on top of the custard. Repeat for the next two layers. Top your creation with a final layer of cake and frost all with buttercream.

Danish Layer Cake #2
Dansk Lagkage

Naomi Carlson, wife of the pastor of Emmaus Lutheran Church of Racine, Wisconsin. This is the mother church of the Danes in Racine.

> 4 eggs, separated
> 2 cups sugar
> 1 teaspoon vanilla
> 1 scant cup milk, scalded
> 2 cups cake flour
> 2 teaspoons baking powder

Beat yolks until thick; add sugar gradually, add vanilla, add stiffly beaten egg whites and continue beating. Add scalded milk, slightly cooled, all at once. Fold in flour to which baking powder has been added. Bake in two 9-inch layer pans at 350° for 12 to 18 minutes.

When cooled, cut each cake into two layers. Put half of the custard filling on the bottom layer. Spread second layer with raspberry jam. Place remainder of custard filling on third layer. Frost top and sides with butter cream icing.

Custard Cream Filling:
> 1/2 cup sugar
> 1/3 cup flour
> 1/2 teaspoon salt
> 1-1/3 cups half-and-half cream
> 1 egg
> 2 tablespoons butter
> 1-1/3 teaspoons vanilla

Mix together in saucepan the sugar, flour, and salt. Stir in cream. It is best to use a heavy pan. Cook over low heat, stirring until mixture boils. Boil 1 minute. Remove from heat. Pour a little of this mixture into 1 slightly beaten large egg. Bring to boiling point. Cool and stir in butter and vanilla.

Butter Cream Icing:
> 3 cups sifted powdered sugar
> 1/3 cup soft butter
> 3 tablespoons cream
> 1-1/2 teaspoons vanilla

Blend sugar and butter together. Stir in cream and vanilla until smooth.

—161

Traditional Danish Wedding Cake
Kransekage

Doris Ericksen Petzke of Racine, Wisconsin, bakes kransekage *for weddings and anniversaries in her community. See photo on page 151.*

1-1/2 pounds almond paste
1-1/2 cups sugar
   3 egg whites, slightly beaten

Crumble almond paste and mix thoroughly with sugar and egg whites. Put through cookie press, filling 18 *kransekage* rings that have been well buttered. Bake at 300° for 20 minutes or until lightly brown.

Frosting:
   1 egg white, beaten frothy
   4 drops vinegar
   enough powdered sugar to make a thin icing

Use decorating tube used for cake-writing to make scallops on top and side of each ring as you assemble the cake tower. To assemble: put frosting on each cake and build like a tower.

Special pans are required for this lovely tower of almond rings. Traditionally the *kransekage* is trimmed with Danish flags, or, when for a wedding, with white doves. Bodil (Mrs. Ron) Johnson of Blair, Nebraska, writes, "A bottle of wine is often placed inside the *kransekage*. At weddings this is the groom's cake."

Variation: Esther Andersen, Dike, Iowa, uses lemon juice instead of vinegar for her icings.

Rice Pudding
Ris a la Mande

Thora Mae Andersen, Solvang, CA

   1 cup rice
   4 cups milk
   8 tablespoons sugar
   1/2 teaspoon salt
1-1/2 to 2 envelopes gelatin
   2 cups whipped cream
   2 teaspoons vanilla
   1/2 cup chopped almonds, optional

Cook rice in milk. Add sugar, salt, and dissolved gelatin. Cool. Add whipped cream and vanilla. Put in a bowl and chill until fairly firm. Serve with cold fruit sauce. (A package of Danish dessert pudding mix makes an excellent sauce.) Sprinkle with nuts. At Christmas time we place one whole almond in the bowl. The finder of the almond in their serving wins a prize.

Rice Pudding with Apples
Risbudding med Æbler

Julie Jensen-McDonald writes, "I like to throw a handful of raisins into the apples as they cook and sprinkle the finished pudding with cinnamon. (Danes will put apples in anything, and it usually works.) This pudding can hide the lucky almond at Christmas time."

1 cup rice
1 quart milk
1/4 cup sugar
   juice of one lemon
   pinch of salt
4 apples, pared and sliced
2 tablespoons cinnamon
   candies
1 tablespoon cornstarch

Cook rice in milk until tender and milk is absorbed. Reserve 2 tablespoons rice. To remainder, add sugar, lemon juice, and salt. Pour and press firmly into a bowl to cool. Pare and thickly slice apples and cook in a little water with cinnamon candies. Drain and cool, reserving liquid. Turn cold rice over onto a large plate. Put apples on top. Thicken liquid from apples with cornstarch, add the reserved rice, and pour around the pudding.

Raspberry Pudding
Hindbærgrød

Eleanor Petersen, Davenport, Iowa

3 cups raspberries
3 cups water
1 cup sugar
3/4 cup potato starch (or corn
   starch)
1/2 cup cold water
   sugar for sprinkling

Bring berries to a boil with 3 cups of water and cook until the seeds separate with the fruit. Add sugar. Stir the starch mixed with 1/2 cup cold water into the boiling, sweetened berry juice. As soon as it thickens, remove from heat and pour into individual glass dishes. Sprinkle with sugar to prevent a skin from forming. Makes six servings.

Variation: Seeds may be strained from the cooked berries if desired. Strawberries, currants, or grape juice may be substituted for the raspberries.

Rhubarb Pudding
Rabarbergrød

Centennial Collection, Ringsted, IA

1-1/2 pounds rhubarb
1-1/2 quarts water
2 cups sugar
6 teaspoons cornstarch
   red food coloring if desired

Cut rhubarb in pieces and cook in water until tender. Press through a sieve to get 4 cups of juice. Discard pulp. Add sugar and coloring. Let it come to a boil, thickening it with cornstarch mixed with a little water. Chill. Serve with thin cream and sugar.

Danish Rum Pudding
Rumfromage

Betty Møllerskov, Racine, Wisconsin. Møllerskov means, in Danish, "miller by the woods." Dagmar Jensen of Clinton, Iowa, also submitted a rum pudding recipe.

4 eggs, separated
1/2 cup sugar
1 envelope unflavored gelatin
1/4 cup water
1-1/2 ounces rum
1/2 pint whipping cream, whipped

Beat egg yolks and sugar until lemon colored. Soak gelatin in 1/4 cup water and melt over hot water. Combine egg yolks and gelatin mixture and add rum. Let stand until it begins to thicken. Fold in stiffly beaten egg whites, then whipped cream. Chill until firm. Serves 12. Serve with raspberry or cherry juice topping.

Sauce:
2 cups juice, raspberry or cherry
1-1/2 teaspoons cornstarch

Heat and let come to a boil and cool. Pour over dessert.

Speech is oft repented silence seldom.
—Danish proverb

Variation: *Genevieve Claussen, a Danish American in Davenport, Iowa, makes berry sauce for Danish rum pudding this way.*

1 pint frozen sweetened red raspberries
1 tablespoon cornstarch
2 tablespoons water

Thaw frozen raspberries and place in covered saucepan. Bring to a boil and simmer 5 minutes. Strain and discard pulp. Blend cornstarch and water and add to the juice, stirring constantly. Cook until mixture boils and thickens. Chill until serving time.

Lemon Cream
Citronfromage

From the good Danish cooks at Ringsted, Iowa

2-1/2 teaspoons unflavored gelatin
1/4 cup cold water
1/2 cup boiling water
1 cup sugar
6 eggs, separated
juice of two lemons
1 lemon rind, grated

Soak unflavored gelatin in 1/4 cup cold water and dissolve in 1/2 cup boiling water. Add sugar. Cool to lukewarm. Beat egg yolks until lemon colored. Stir into gelatin mixture. Add lemon juice and grated lemon rind. Fold in stiffly beaten egg whites. Pour into large bowl and chill. This is good with fruit sauce or whipped cream.

Farmer Lass with Veil
Bondepige med Slør

This recipe comes from the late Mette Marie Ibsen Faurschou, Harlan, Iowa, grandmother of the author who comments, "Danes will sweeten almost anything with remarkably interesting results."

2 to 3 slices pumpernickel bread, to make about 1 heaping cup of crumbs
1/2 cup brown sugar
3 tablespoons butter raspberry or strawberry jam, or thick applesauce
1 cup whipping cream, whipped

Dry pumpernickel in a 200° oven or air dry. Crush bread finely with a rolling pin. Mix heaping cup of crumbs with brown sugar. Melt butter in a skillet and add the crumbs and sugar, browning them over low heat. Stir often, watching them carefully. When they are lightly browned, place one layer of the mixture in a bowl, cover with jam or applesauce, and the rest of the crumbs and sugar. Cool, top with whipped cream, and serve.

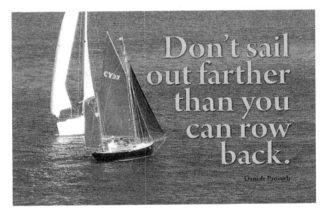

Available from Penfield Books
in postcard or magnet
This ship in Copenhagen Harbour, Denmark,
was photographed by Dale Edwards
of Fort Collins, Colorado.

Appetizers

Salads

Vegetables

Main Dishes

Soups

Breads

*Hans Christian Andersen
paper cut from Penfield Books
in postcard or magnet*

CPSIA information can be obtained at www.ICGtesting.com
Printed in the USA
LVOW04s0838050515

437257LV00034B/882/P